Crispin Hayhoe is a practising barrister who regularly deals with Child Support cases and has done so for almost 20 years. As a qualified accountant and former Licenced Insolvency Practitioner as well as a lawyer he is able to give focused and highly cost-effective advice to clients. Crispin is the first-choice advocate for the Child Maintenance Service for its high profile cases, some of which have been reported in the national media.

A Practical Guide to Applications and Hearings in the Magistrates and County Courts in Relation to the Child Maintenance Service

A Practical Guide to Applications and Hearings in the Magistrates and County Courts in Relation to the Child Maintenance Service

Crispin Hayhoe,

Barrister Lincoln's Inn,

MA (Hons), PGDL, FCCA

Law Brief Publishing

Published 2023 by Law Brief Publishing, an imprint of Law Brief Publishing Ltd
30 The Parks
Minehead
Somerset
TA24 8BT

www.lawbriefpublishing.com

Paperback: 978-1-914608-29-2

To

Anne, Sarah, Benedict, & Sam

PREFACE

In the 30 odd years since its introduction the Child Support Act 1991 and the child support regime have undergone considerable revision moving from a fairly toothless system to one where driving licences, passports and even personal liberty are at risk.

The Child Maintenance Service now has extensive investigatory powers, exercisable administratively, as well as the ability to require the disclosure of personal information (not just from the Paying Person but also their bankers, accountants and advisors) and to effectively freeze bank accounts.

Against the background this book aims to provide in a single concise volume invaluable guidance for practitioners as to how to navigate the Child Support system where it interacts with the Courts. The author believes that it fairly states the law as at 31 March 2023.

With particular thanks to Anita, Annie, Diane, Frances, Gill, Jim, Judy, Lata, Penny, Pradip, & Teresa. Thank you for all your help and guidance over the years without which this book would not have been possible.

Crispin Hayhoe
August 2023

PREFACE

CONTENTS

List of Abbreviations

Introduction		1
Chapter One	Claims – Calculation/Assessment	7
Chapter Two	Paternity	31
Chapter Three	At Court	37
Chapter Four	Information Offences	41
Chapter Five	Deduction From Earnings Order	51
Chapter Six	Regular and Lump Sum Deduction Orders	65
Chapter Seven	Liability Orders	81
Chapter Eight	Set-Aside Applications	99
Chapter Nine	Sanctions	105
Chapter Ten	County Court Hearings	131
Chapter Eleven	Other "Defences" And Issues Arising in Child Maintenance Cases	135
Chapter Twelve	Complaints and Appeals	139

LIST OF ABBREVIATIONS

CMEC	Child Maintenance & Enforcement Commission
CMS	Child Maintenance Service
CPO	Court Presenting Officer
CSA	Child Support Agency
DEO	Deduction from Earnings Order
DMD	Default Maintenance Decision
FLSDO	Final Lump Sum Deduction Order
LO	Liability Order
LSDO	Lump Sum Deduction Order
MA	Maintenance Assessment
MC	Maintenance Calculation
MEF	Means Enquiry Form
MIMO	Money In Money Out form
NRP	Non-Resident Person
PP	Paying Person
PwC	Person with Care
QC	Qualifying Child
RDO	Regular Deduction Order
ROC	Relevant Other Child
RP	Receiving Parent
SAR	Subject Access Request

INTRODUCTION

Terminology

The author does not wish, in any way, to be tendentious and will use the terminology of the relevant legislation which is Receiving Person ("RP") or Person with Care ("PwC") for the recipient of child maintenance and Paying Person ("PP") or Non-Resident Person ("NRP") for the payer of maintenance.

It should be recognised that the vast bulk of PP/NRPs are men, and the vast bulk of RP/PwCs are women. While cases which get to court are a relatively small subsection of the total number of child maintenance cases and the author's experience is not a scientific sample perhaps in 1 in 200 cases is the PP/NRP a woman.

While shared care arrangements are commonplace, (and there are many instances when teenage children mostly live with their fathers), the bulk of the responsibility for looking after children and, as a consequence, the major entitlement to child maintenance, rests with the mothers. One of the key indicators used in assessing both the ongoing entitlement to maintenance and who is to be the recipient is the payment of Child Benefit.

Origin of Child Maintenance Service

In the late 1980s there was a general dissatisfaction with how children of divorced or separated couples, or indeed couples which had never been formally married but were no longer together, were maintained. There was a perception that absent fathers (for it was usually fathers) would leave the family home and refuse to take any financial responsibility for their children.

When the courts were involved there appeared to be a good deal of inconsistency in terms of the orders which were made. Some orders were for trivial amounts, and it was difficult and time-consuming to get orders varied. When substantive orders had been made it was often costly and difficult to enforce them.

It seemed that some mothers were content to collect benefits rather than seek to pursue the fathers for maintenance and some absent fathers would be earning good money but not paying their way. Although there was a unit within the Department for Social Security which was tasked with pursuing such absent fathers its impact was limited. The burden had shifted to the state.

As is so often the case there were stories in the press and media about the situation and there was a general feeling that "something must be done".

It was against this background that the Child Support Act 1991 ("the Act") came into being and established the Child Support Agency ("CSA"). It was intended that the CSA would be an independent body who would impartially calculate a fair level of child maintenance which would be acceptable to both the PwC and the NRP. Unfortunately, as those readers who practice in the Family Courts will be only too well aware, some relationship breakdowns do not engender any equanimity or reasonableness.

The nature of the regime established by the act was helpfully characterised by the then LJ Hale in the case of *Huxley v Child Support Officer [2000] 1 FLR 898, 908* where she said:

> *"The child support system has elements of private and public law but fundamentally it is a nationalised system for assessing and enforcing an obligation which each parent owes primarily to the child. It replaces the powers of the courts, which can no longer make orders for periodical payments for children save in very limited circumstances. Unless she can secure a voluntary agreement at least as high as that which the CSA would assess, the PwC is expected to look to the Agency to assess her child support according to the formula, whether or not she is on benefit. The fact that it does her no direct good if she is on means-tested*

benefits, and that much CSA activity so far has been in relation to parents on benefit, does not alter the fundamental characteristics of the scheme."

Development

When the CSA came into being it seems to have been assumed that absent fathers would be relatively happy to cooperate with it to maintain their children and this was certainly the position for most. Part of the initial focus was in ensuring that mothers claiming benefits, rather than seeking a contribution from the absent father, were compelled to cooperate with the CSA to identify and locate the NRP. This compulsion, pursuant to section 6 of the Act, remained in force until July 2008. There was also provision that in the event that maintenance was recovered from a NRP some of this could be clawed back for the benefit of the Secretary of State.

There have been three substantive sets of rules for the calculation of the maintenance to be paid by the PP/NRP. The initial rules were complex and inflexible and involved consideration of both the PP/PwC's and the RP/NRP's income. This lack of flexibility led to delays and some unfair results. Campaigning by organisations such as Fathers for Justice challenged the application of the rules.

It also became clear that some NRPs were not going to cooperate with the CSA and the reforms needed to be introduced to compel such individuals to pay the maintenance due. Over the last 30 years there has been a consistent trend to increase the powers of the CSA and its successor organisations to access information from other bodies, both governmental and non-governmental and to increase its powers to recover maintenance due.

There has also been a trend to try and simplify the methodology for calculating the maintenance due. When the legislation was originally introduced it was hoped that this would result in a saving to taxpayers however the costs of operating the system both in respect of the performance of maintenance calculations and the collection thereof means that the hoped-for savings do not appear to have been realised. The most recent trend is now to encourage PP/NRPs and RP/PwCs to use CMS/CSA to calculate the maintenance due but to have the payments made by the PP/NRP directly to the RP/PwC without the CMS/CSA becoming an intermediary (so-called "Direct Pay"). Of course, there are a number of cases where the PP/NRP is reluctant to make payment and in those circumstances CMS/CSA continues to be involved in recovering money from the PP/NRP and paying it to the RP/PwC ("Collect and Pay" in the jargon).

Covid pandemic

The Covid pandemic had a significant impact on the operation of the CMS. The need to process a huge increase in the claims for universal credit and other state support led to the redeployment of staff from CMS/CSA to processing benefit claims.

This meant that there was a 6 to 9-month period where there was a virtual standstill in the processing of CMS/CSA cases be it in making maintenance calculations or taking enforcement action.

Staff have now been returned to their original duties and efforts are being made to clear the backlog of cases.

CMS / CSA role and individual parental rights

One of the features of CMS/CSA being an independent body is that it becomes the "prosecuting authority". RP/PwCs have no power or standing to take any actions to compel the PP/NRP to comply with the child maintenance obligations pursuant to the Act. (There are some circumstances when there are residual rights of action which are outwith the framework of the Act, these usually relate to cases where the income / wealth of the PP/NRP is above the upper threshold used in maintenance calculations). The Act confers no right of recovery or enforcement on the RP/PwC. This was definitively determined in the case of *Regina v.*

Secretary of State for Work and Pensions (Respondent) ex parte Kehoe [2005] UKHL 48. Lord Hope of Craighead made this clear in paragraph 35 where he said:

> *"I would conclude that the 1991 Act has deliberately avoided conferring a right on the person with care to enforce a child maintenance assessment against the absent parent. Enforcement is exclusively a matter for the Secretary of State."*

The consequence of this is that the RP/PwC is dependent on CMS/CSA to assess and secure any child maintenance due.

Case longevity

Readers may be slightly surprised that reference is made to the child maintenance regime as it operated in the late 1990s and early 2000s. It might very reasonably be assumed that monies owed from so long ago would not be recoverable as a result of the provisions of the Limitation Act 1980. However, child support debt occupies a very particular place in English law as, save for debt rising prior to 12 July 2000, the Limitation Act has been disapplied.

Similarly, child support debt, is not extinguished by a bankruptcy or other insolvency proceeding. This means that somebody can still be pursued through the courts, and otherwise, in respect of a child support debt that arose more than 20 years ago, notwithstanding the fact that they may have been made bankrupt several times in the interim.

CHAPTER ONE

CLAIMS – CALCULATION / ASSESSMENT

How does a claim start?

Claims are usually started by the RP/PwC making a claim to CMS/CSA for child maintenance. It used to be the case that if the RP/PwC was receiving benefits from the state that they could be compelled to make a child maintenance application. This compulsion was removed by the Child Maintenance and Other Payments Act 2008 ("CMOP") with effect from 27 October 2008.

Claimants can both be the RP/PwC and/or the RP/NRP. It is sometimes the case that the RP/NRP wishes to involve CMS/CSA because the amount of maintenance that will be payable under CMS/CSA rules is less than might be payable pursuant to a court order.

Today potential claimants are required to engage with Get Help Arranging Child Maintenance before a claim is made to CMS/CSA. This facility sets out basic details as to how CMS/CSA works. It also makes it clear that fees will be charged if CMS/CSA is involved in quantifying child maintenance. There would also appear to be a steer to try and have parents agree maintenance between themselves rather than involving CMS/CSA. This process tries to make provision for situations where there is some risk or danger in the PP/NRP being in direct contact with the RP/PwC or having knowledge of the RP/PwC's location. While it is clear that the authorities are mindful of the dangers posed by some PP/NRPs if one was of a cynical turn of mind, it might be that this process was perceived as being aimed, in part, at diverting people away from CMS/CSA if reasonably possible.

Jurisdiction

CMS/CSA has the power to quantify/order the payment of child maintenance when the following conditions are met:

- there is a qualifying child who is either under 16 years of age or
- if 16 or older, (but less than 20) and child benefit is payable in relation to them, and they are in full-time education (but not university or university standard education);
- there is a RP/PwC who provides day-to-day care for the qualifying child;
- there is a PP/NRP; and
- the qualifying child(ren), the RP/PwC and the PP/NRP are all habitually resident in the UK.

The term "habitually resident" is not defined in the legislation. Case law suggests that it is equivalent to domicile for tax purposes. Every such case is fact specific but the gist would appear to be that unless one of the parents (or conceivably the child) has permanently moved abroad they will remain "habitually resident" in the UK.

There are further circumstances where even if PP/NRP is not "habitually resident" in the UK that CMS/CSA is entitled to make a maintenance calculation. These are if the PP/NRP is:

- a member of the Armed Forces;
- an employee of the civil service;

- an employee of a UK registered company working outside the UK (whose pay calculations and administration are performed in the UK); and

- it is an employee of various health bodies including the NHS, a local authority, or other similar body.

If the above provisions do not apply to the PP/NRP then the Family Court may retain a residual authority to make an order in respect of maintenance or other financial provision for the child. The enforcement of such an order would not be within the purview of CMS/CSA.

Maintenance calculation

The rules for making a maintenance calculation, or as it used to be termed maintenance assessment, have evolved since the inception of CMS/CSA. There are three frameworks which have been applied to make the calculation. Old rules, the New Rules and the 2012 rules. The key features of each of these regimes are set out below:

Old Rules:

- These rules were administered by the CSA acting on behalf of the Department for Work and Pensions.

- The income of both the RP/PwC and the PP/NRP was taken into account in the calculation.

- From 1996 there was some scope to vary the calculation by way of a departure direction. This allowed maintenance to be increased to reflect underused assets, lifestyle and a diversion of income.

- There was a reduction in the assessment for what was termed "Shared Care" if the QC(s) spent more than 52 nights a year with the PP/NRP.

- Generally, no fees were payable by either the PP/NRP or the RP/PwC.

- The rules were complex and overly prescriptive in an effort to be fair.

New rules:

- These rules were administered by the CSA on behalf of what was then the Child Maintenance and Enforcement Commission ("CMEC").

- The maintenance calculation, as it was now termed, was based on a percentage of the PP/NRP's net income alone. No consideration was given to the income of the RP/PwC.

- The system of variations to the standard rules had been expanded slightly to include income which had previously not been taken into account such as dividends.

- The Shared Care reduction remained.

- As with the Old Rules there was generally no charge for the work done by CMS/CSA.

- The methodology was simplified with the aim of reducing the complexity involved in making a maintenance calculation.

2012 rules:

- There was a change in terminology with Non-Resident Parents ("NRPs") becoming Paying Parents ("PP") and Persons/Parents with Care ("PwCs") becoming Receiving Person/Parents ("RPs").

- The formula for calculating the maintenance payable was further simplified to be a percentage of the NRP/PP's gross income. The RP/PwC's income remained outside the calculation.

- If it was agreed that there would be Shared Care it was assumed that the 52 nights a year threshold applied. If care was shared equally then there would be no maintenance calculation.

- There continue to be variations / adjustments in respect of unearned income and if income had been diverted away from the PP/NRP. Importantly the possibility of adjustment on the basis that the PP/NRP had a lifestyle inconsistent with their reported income was abandoned.

- The regime in respect of charges was substantially altered. Flat fees for making an application were introduced, there was a 20% charge in respect of the maintenance payable for the PP/NRP and a 4% charge on the maintenance collected payable by the RP/PwC if the collect and pay service was being used. Deduction from Earnings Orders and Regular Deduction Orders would attract a fee of £50, Lump Sum Deduction orders would have a fee of £200 and Liability Order applications would have a fee of £300. The relatively high level of fees, certainly in relation to what had gone before, was intended to encourage parents to come to their own arrangements in respect of maintenance rather than engaging CMS/CSA in its collection and payment.

- There would be annual reviews of the maintenance calculation but absent a very substantial change (greater than 25%) in circumstances it was difficult to alter the calculation within the year. Some view this as a sensible reform avoiding the cost of minor changes to a maintenance calculation while others view this as inflexibly requiring the payment of higher level of maintenance when the income to justify it is no longer earned.

Key features and consequences of the changes

When the child support regime was set up in 1992 there was a general concern to avoid an arm of the state being able to pry into the minutiae of people's lives and a desire to be scrupulously fair in calculating the maintenance assessment. This resulted in a system where the process of making an assessment was laborious and complex and the ability to obtain relevant information from other government sources was heavily curtailed, if not non-existent. Powers to gather information, to investigate financial circumstances and to enforce compliance were minimal or non-existent.

Over the last 30 years there has been a trend to significantly increase the information gathering, investigatory and enforcement powers. At the same time there has been an effort to simplify the process of making a maintenance calculation recognising that this may result in some unfairness.

One of the major reforms has been to allow CMS/CSA to have effectively direct access to the HMRC systems so that they can see what level of income has been reported by the PP/NRP on a real-time basis. The interaction between the systems has not always been perfect but it is a great improvement on what went before.

CMS/CSA is now able to require information from banks and employers and other institutions in respect of the finances and earnings of NRP/PPs. Indeed, the failure to provide information is now itself an offence pursuant to section 14A of the Act.

Making the maintenance calculation

Making the maintenance calculation is a six-stage process.

The first stage – income

The first step is to consider the PP/NRP's income.

- CMS/CSA have a number of methods for obtaining information about the PP/NRP's income. This usually requires the cooperation of the PP/NRP. It used to be that a Means Enquiry Form ("MEF") would be sent to the father and this form would have a series of questions about his income and expenses.

- Over time the information gathered has been simplified. There is an increasing use of online tools to gather this information, but it can still be supplemented by telephone calls and paper-based forms.

- As noted above it is also possible for CMS/CSA to obtain information directly from HMRC and this is the usual primary source of information, but it is also possible for CMS/CSA to obtain information direct from the employer or a third party such as an accountant.

- The focus is usually on the annual taxable gross income.

- It is also possible for CMS/CSA to confirm whether benefits are being paid to the PP/NRP.

- If the PP/NRP disagrees with the income figure used, then they have the option to provide information / evidence as to why the figure is incorrect. If the information provided yields a difference the maintenance payable of more than 25% then CMS/CSA should be prepared to vary their calculation. If the error is less than 25% then CMS/CSA is unlikely to vary the calculation.

- If the PP/NRP's income is more than £3000 per week (£156,000 pa) earnings above this threshold will be ignored in making the maintenance calculation. It is potentially open to the PP/PwC to make an application to the Family Court if they believe that additional maintenance is justified.

- If the PP/NRP is in receipt of benefits, then the usual assessment is a flat rate of maintenance of £7 per week.

- If for some reason CMS/CSA is unable to obtain the necessary information to make a full maintenance calculation it is able to make a maintenance calculation using what is known as the best evidence assessment or a Default Maintenance Decision ("DMD") (s12 of the Act). The best evidence assessment uses information from various research, surveys and databases such as the Annual Survey of Hours and Earnings. The DMD is a series of flat rate figures being £39 a week for one child, £51 a week for two children and £64 a week for three or more children.

- The rates for the DMD are set at a level which are designed to encourage the PP/NRP to provide information so as to enable a full maintenance calculation to be performed. But readers will appreciate that for some higher earners they may choose to try and limit information about their income and financial circumstances on the basis that paying a DMD is less than would be payable if the true position were known. There is a substantial risk in taking this course of action in that if either as a result of an appeal or some other information gathering exercise the true position becomes known the DMD can be set aside and the corrected figure can become payable and back dated.

The second stage – variation

The second stage is to consider whether there are any matters which might affect the level of assessable income. Included within this category are pension payments or financial obligations in respect of other children. Pension payments to an occupational or personal pension scheme are usually deducted from the income figure in deriving the taxable gross annual income. Additional sources of income may also be considered at this stage. These considerations are known as a "variation".

The PP/NRP can ask for special expenses to be taken into account with the effect of potentially reducing the taxable income on which maintenance is assessed. These can include:

- Costs associated with keeping in touch with the Qualifying Child. For instance, if it is necessary to spend more than £10 a week on petrol to travel between the PP/NRP's home and where the child is living.

- Repaying debts which were incurred during the relationship. A typical example is payments in respect of a car loan or similar agreement in relation to a vehicle the RP/PwC is using. Again, there is a minimum threshold of £10 per week.

- Boarding school fees are another potentially permissible expense. These often become the subject of dispute between the PP/NRP and the RP/PwC. It is not unusual for both parties to have been in favour of the expense of private education during the relationship only for one party or the other to change their view when the relationship breaks down. The potential deduction is limited to costs in relation to the boarding of the school fees. There is a £10 per week minimum.

- Costs connected with supporting a child with special needs or chronic or long-term illness who lives with the PP/NRP (or their new partner) can trigger a reduction in the assessable income.

- Property costs (usually a mortgage, loan or insurance policy) in relation to a property occupied by the PP/NRP and the Qualifying Child can give rise to a deduction. These expenses must relate to a property which used to be occupied both by the PP/NRP and the RP/PwC and the PP/NRP should have no legal or beneficial interest in the property. The £10 per week threshold applies.

Special expenses will not be considered if the PP/NRP is in receipt of benefits or has a gross income of less than £7 per week.

In considering potential additional income sources there are three basic categories that will be assessed. First, what is termed "unearned" income, this is usually dividends and interest arising from savings or investments and also includes rental income from property assets. If the income is less than £2500 per year it will be discounted.

Secondly, if there is "earned" income of more than £100 per week, where the PP/NRP, or their new partner, has receipts from a pension or employment or self-employment or taxable benefits.

Thirdly, if there has been a "diversion" of income. Some individuals are in the position that they can direct how they receive, or do not receive, their income. It is not unknown for PP/NRPs to arrange for income to be paid to a friend or family member rather than directly to themselves. In so doing they seek to suppress their level of income and maintenance liability. This is potentially a very risky course of action as it might involve giving false information to HM Revenue & Customs and possibly an evasion of tax.

The issue of having a "lifestyle" over and above that which would be supported by the reported level of income has, in the past, been a basis for a variation in the maintenance calculation. As matters presently stand this lifestyle inconsistency is not subject to investigation by CMS/CSA. However, it is possible that this position will change as a result of legislative proposals currently being considered by the government.

When considering whether or not to make a variation, be it to increase or decrease the base income, CMS/CSA in addition to considering the factual basis for the variation is also required to consider whether or not it is "just and equitable" to make the change. This is effectively a catchall provision allowing a measure of discretion to be applied.

If a request for a variation is made the basis for the variation and the information provided in support of it will be disclosed to the other party. The other party will be entitled to make representations to CMS/CSA in relation to the proposed variation and depending on the decision by CMS/CSA it is a matter which can be referred to the Independent Appeals Tribunal in the event that one, or other, of the parties believes the decision is wrong.

The third stage – child maintenance rate

Having determined the weekly level of income assessable to child maintenance a child maintenance rate will be applied to the figure to determine the weekly maintenance payable. There are five bands of maintenance. They are as follows:

Nil	for incomes less than £7 per week.
Flat	for incomes between £7 and £100 (or if benefits are being paid).
Reduced	for incomes between £100.01 and £199.99.
Basic	for incomes between £200 and £800 per week.
Basic Plus	for incomes between £800.01 to £3000. The first tranche of income up to the £800 is assessed using the Basic rate.

The fourth stage – number of children to be taken into account

Having determined the rate of child maintenance payable CMS/CSA then moves to consider how many children should be taken into account. This can become quite complicated as the PP/NRP may have other children living with them and for whom they are financially responsible. These may be the PP/NRP's biological children or children of a new partner. There may also be children for whom the PP/NRP is financially responsible/liable from another relationship. These children may be subject to a maintenance calculation or another family-based maintenance arrangement (be it one ordered by a court, or one negotiated by the parties themselves).

Maintenance liabilities which can be considered at this stage can include monies payable in respect of children living abroad.

<u>The fifth stage – weekly amount of child maintenance</u>

Having determined the assessable income and the number of children to be taken into account CMS/CSA will move to work out the weekly amount of child maintenance payable.

If the Basic Rate of maintenance is payable then this will be 12% of the gross weekly income for one child, 16% for two children and 19% for three or more children.

If the Basic Rate Plus of maintenance is payable then there will be an additional 9% of the gross weekly income between £800 and £3000 if there is one child, there will be an additional 12% of gross weekly income between £800 and £3000 if there are two children, and if there are three or more children there will be an additional 15% payable in respect of the income between £800 and £3000.

If the Reduced Rate of maintenance is payable then there is a liability of £7 a week in respect of the first £100 of income and a percentage charge in respect of the remainder of their weekly income. The supplementary percentage is 17% if there is one child, 25% if there are two and 31% if there are three. There are further adjustments if the PP/NRP is also financially responsible (though not paying formal maintenance) other children.

The flat rate of £7 is payable if the PP/NRP has a gross weekly income of £100 or less or is in receipt of benefits. There is a long list of eligible/trigger benefits. In most cases information about the payment of benefits will be passed to CMS/CSA automatically though there are some rare cases where a PP/NRP may be receiving benefit on behalf of another in which case this would need to be disclosed to CMS/CSA.

The nil rate band applies when the PP/NRP

- Has gross income of less than £7 per week,
- is under 16 years of age,
- is between 16 and 19 and is in certain classes of full-time education / training
- is a 16 or 17-year old in receipt of certain types of benefit
- is in prison,
- or is in a care home or independent hospital and receiving help with fees.

It should be noted that it is the responsibility of the PP/NRP to advise CMS/CSA of any change in circumstances which includes being subject to a custodial sentence. The author is aware of cases where PP/NRPs have been in prison for years but despite having no income, have continued to accrue child maintenance debt because they have failed to advise CMS/CSA of their incarceration.

<u>The sixth stage – shared care</u>

If there is shared care between the PP/NRP and the RP/PwC then this can result in a reduction in the maintenance payable in respect of the Basic Rate, Basic Rate Plus, and Reduced Rate bands. If the PP/NRP has shared care for between 52 and 103 nights there is a 1/7 reduction; if the shared care is between 104 and 155 nights there is a 2/7 reduction; if the shared care is between 156 and 174 nights then there is a 3/7 reduction and if shared care is for more than 170 nights there is a 50% reduction plus a further £7 a week reduction for each child.

CMS/CSA recognise that the number of nights of shared care may vary and it is not necessary to report all such variations but if a variation means crossing one of the thresholds above then this should be notified at once. If it is not, and it would result in a reduction in what was to be paid, then this reduction will not take effect. Increases as a result of a change in living arrangements may be back dated.

Fees

There are two models for determining and paying child maintenance. One is "Direct Pay" and the other is "Collect and Pay".

If the Direct Pay model is used, then the maintenance should be paid from the PP/NRP to the RP/PwC without the involvement of CMS/CSA. Under this system no fees are payable[1].

Alternatively, if the Collect and Pay system is used, the money is paid by the PP/NRP to CMS/CSA who in turn pass the money onto the RP. If this system is used CMS/CSA will charge both the PP/NRP and the RP a fee for its involvement. The PP/NRP is required to pay an additional 20% of the maintenance payable by way of a fee (so the PP/NRP's fee increases the amount to be paid by 1/5). The RP/PwC also has to pay a fee which is 4% of the maintenance received. This is deducted by CMS/CSA from the payment made to the RP/PwC. The fees together represent almost one quarter of the maintenance payable.

These fees appear to be intended, at least in part, to provide a financial incentive for the parents to agree to use the Direct Pay system rather than to engage CMS/CSA in the collection and payment of maintenance. It would appear that the process of collecting and paying maintenance is expensive and bureaucratic and that the government wishes to minimise the costs of the system by encouraging a do-it-yourself solution. The author is aware of instances where the PP/NRP has not paid all that is owed and built-up significant arrears such that enforcement action if

1 Save that there is a one off £20 fee for doing the maintenance calculation.

being taken and yet they are returned to the Direct Pay system. The rationale for such decisions is somewhat opaque.

Mandatory reconsideration

If either the PP/NRP or the RP/PwC is unhappy with the proposed maintenance calculation they are able to challenge it by asking for the decision to be reviewed internally by CMS/CSA. This process is known as mandatory reconsideration. The right to seek this revision applies to both the payer and the payee. Not infrequently both parties to seek to have the same calculation adjusted in their favour.

Human nature means that it is by no means unusual for parties to seek to pay less or receive more. Without wishing to be trite the chances of success in respect of a mandatory reconsideration will be significantly improved if evidence can be provided to support the proposed change. It is surprising how many cases which subsequently reach enforcement proceedings have been the subject to applications for mandatory reconsideration where evidence of payments of child support or variations to income, or additional unreported sources of income, have been promised but not delivered. It would appear, at least on some occasions, that PP/NRPs make applications for mandatory reconsideration purely as a delaying tactic. In that the liability for maintenance will continue to accrue even while the application is being considered the consequence of this tactic is simply to increase the debt.

An application for a mandatory reconsideration must be made within 32 days of the date of the letter telling the party as to the outcome of the maintenance calculation.

If the mandatory reconsideration results in a variation of the maintenance calculation this will in turn trigger further appeal rights.

Supersession pursuant to s17 of the Act

The Secretary of State now has authority, in certain circumstances, to supersede / replace an existing maintenance calculation.

The regulations relating to this section are the *Child Support Maintenance Calculation Regulations 2012/2677*.

The regulations set out the grounds for a supersession. The first ground is that that there has been a relevant change of circumstance since the decision had affect or it is expected that a relevant change of circumstances will occur. The second is that the decision was made in ignorance of, or was based on, a mistake as to some material fact. The third is that the decision was wrong in law (this ground is not open to be raised if the decision was made by an appeal tribunal).

This is an important provision as it allows the Secretary of State to go behind the maintenance calculation in certain circumstances. A formal application under section 28G of the Act should be made. Further details of this process are set out in sections 28A to G of the Act. They allow the Secretary of State to reject the application after a preliminary review and to impose a payment condition pending the completion of the exercise. If the payment condition is not honoured then this can allow the Secretary of State to dismiss the application with out further consideration. There used to be provision to appeal decisions to the First Teir Tribunal but this provision has been repealed.

Annual review

As a result of what is known as the 2012 reforms an annual review of the maintenance calculation has been instituted. This is a normal process but reference to the "review" has sometimes caused confusion in courts considering various stages of the enforcement of the payment of maintenance leading the court to believe that there is some question as to the validity of existing maintenance calculations when there is not. All that is happening is that CMS/CSA is looking to see if there should be a change in the maintenance payable going forward. It is prospective not retrospective.

It would appear that the aim of this process has been to curtail the ability of, primarily, PP/NRPs to seek a change to the maintenance calculation on the basis of a relatively minor change in circumstances. The general rule is that unless there has been a change in income of more than 25% this will be ignored until the annual review.

The annual review, which arises on the 12-month anniversary of the notification to the/NRP of the making of the maintenance application, works by CMS/CSA obtaining information from HM Revenue and Customs as to the PP/NRP's income (though information can be gathered from the employer or an accountant) and performing the maintenance calculation as described above.

The revised (if it is revised) calculation is notified to the PP/NRP and the RP/PwC and they are told what is due to be paid over the coming 12 months. This notification includes details of the income used (and any other relevant information perhaps in relation to unearned income). Once the outcome of the annual review has been notified to both the PP/NRP and the RP/PwC they have 20 days to make representations. If parties are unhappy with the response to any representations this can in turn trigger a mandatory reconsideration and potentially a right to appeal to the independent tribunal.

Notification of changes in circumstances

If either parent's circumstances change this can result in an obligation to advise CMS/CSA of the change.

For PP/NRPs they must advise of changes in income in particular if it rises by more than 25%. (Much of the literature and guidance provided by the DWP talks about rises in income. Of course, if income falls by 25% or more this would trigger a review of the current level of maintenance just as much as the increase in income does.) There is also an obligation to notify CMS/CSA if income rises by £7 per week or more and the person is on the nil rate of child maintenance. This change of circumstance needs to be notified within 14 days of the change coming into effect[2].

If the PP/NRP changes employment this must be notified within seven days.

If the PP/NRP changes address then this must be notified to the Secretary of State within seven days.[3]

If child maintenance is being gathered via a Deduction from Earnings Order and the PP/NRP moves to a new employer then the following information must be provided:

- name and address of new employer;
- the expected level of earnings;
- any new payroll number or identification;
- the type of work that is being done; and
- the new address at which the person is working.

If the PP/NRP moves to a new residential address this change must be notified.

The change in circumstances should be notified to CMS/CSA within seven days and a failure to do so can result in a fine of up to £1000.

Additionally, CMS/CSA should be advised in the event that:

---

2 Child Support Information Regulations 2008/2551, reg. 9A

3 Child Support Information Regulations 2008/2551, reg. 9

- a Qualifying Child leaves full-time, non-advanced education or approved training, gets married, or enters into a civil partnership;
- anyone involved in the child maintenance case dies; and/or
- if the present arrangement for payment is Collect & Pay and they wish to move to a Direct Pay.

The RP/PwC also has an obligation to notify CMS/CSA in respect of the following changes:

- a qualifying child (or children) ceases to live with the RP/PwC such that this would mean that the PP/NRP no longer has an obligation to pay child maintenance;
- anyone involved in the child maintenance case dies;
- there is a change in the contact details;
- there is a change in personal information and or bank or building society details;
- they want to move from Direct Pay to Collect & Pay or vice versa.

Appeal

If as a result of the mandatory consideration referred to above one of the parties is unhappy with the result they can potentially appeal it to the First-Tier Tribunal. The letter providing details of the outcome of the mandatory reconsideration should contain details about making the appeal. In general the tribunal will not consider an appeal unless the mandatory reconsideration process has been undertaken.

There are tight time limits for the making of any appeal to the tribunal and in the event that it they are not completed in proper time an appeal with merit may not be heard.

The appeal tribunal usually consists of a District Judge assisted by an accountant. There is a good deal of discretion as to how the proceedings are conducted. In general, it will be a tripartite arrangement with both the PP/NRP and the RP/PwC being able to make submissions as well as CMS/CSA. If there is a dispute about the PP/NRP's income or financial circumstances more generally they may be ordered to give disclosure of relevant documents and information. Similarly other parties may be entitled to provide evidence / documentation in support of their positions to the tribunal. CMS/CSA will prepare a briefing document for the tribunal explaining the rationale for the decision which it has reached.

If the tribunal makes a decision which one of the parties thinks is wrong there is a right of appeal, on a matter of law, to the second tier tribunal. The process that this is not straightforward as the initial stage is to invite the first-tier Tribunal to reconsider the decision it has just made and to consider whether there is a matter of law which merits consideration by the second-tier tribunal. This usually requires that the reasons for the first-tier Tribunal's decision have been set out before the matter can advance to the second tier.

Continuing role for the courts

While in general the effect of the child support legislation has been to pass control over the quantification and enforcement of payment of child maintenance from the courts to CMS/CSA there remain a few discrete areas where the courts continue to have a role.

The first of these is where CMS/CSA does not have jurisdiction to act. Usually this will mean that one of the parties is not ordinarily resident in the United Kingdom. Each case will depend on its individual facts but there can be circumstances where the courts will consider that they have jurisdiction which falls out with the statutory jurisdiction given to CMS/CSA.

Other examples can be when the child in question is a stepchild or no longer meets the definition of "qualifying child" as set out in the legislation but would still be entitled to maintenance (possibly as a result of disability). Sometimes there will be an application for the RP/PwC to pay maintenance.

If the parties agree a child maintenance order/settlement agreement by consent then this will continue to be valid. If a practitioner is involved in making such an agreement it would be prudent for them to ensure that it contains provisions to deal with the situation where a subsequent application may be made to CMS/CSA for child maintenance. One commonplace provision is that any monies due to be paid under the negotiated agreement are reduced on a pound for pound basis in the event that there is a CMS/CSA child maintenance calculation.

An area where the court continues to retain jurisdiction is in relation to orders for educational expenses. In the vast majority of cases this will be in relation to the payment of school fees but in particular cases the scope can be wider. Similarly, the court can make orders in relation to costs attributable to a child's disability.

The court also retains jurisdiction to make what is known as a top up order. These generally only apply when the PP/NRP has a gross income in excess of £3000 per week or £156,000 per year. In such cases the attitude of the respective parties may be, to say the least, fractious and there may be a dispute as to whether or not the PP/NRP's income is above the relevant threshold. There is competing judicial authority as to whether or not the court can act if CMS/CSA has yet to formally assess the PP/NRP's income as being above the relevant threshold. If income is above this threshold then it is ignored by CMS/CSA, but may be considered by the court. In such circumstances the CMS/CSA orders in respect of child maintenance remain valid and enforceable and there is simply an extra layer imposed by the court.

Once CMS/CSA has made a maintenance calculation this will, by operation of law, automatically bring to an end any court order for maintenance unless it meets one of the exceptions identified above (basically educational or disability related orders). The court order will cease to have effect on the effective date of the maintenance calculation. Care needs to be taken that provisions of the court order which go beyond the maintenance calculation (for instance in relation to funding of university or other tertiary education) are not lost when the maintenance calculation is made. One way to deal with this would be to have a separate freestanding agreement to cover such non-CMS/CSA related expenses. Another method of countering this potential problem is to provide that the court order only becomes active when CMS/CSA ceases to have jurisdiction / authority.

If a party, or parties, wish to mitigate the potential impact of a CMS/CSA maintenance calculation on their negotiated settlement this can be done by simply providing that maintenance between the parties will be determined in the same way as would have been done by CMS/CSA. Indeed, in that such a privately negotiated arrangement would avoid the fees being charged by CMS/CSA there would be a financial incentive for both parties to go down this route. It is also worth noting that by virtue of being a statutory scheme the level of maintenance that would be assessed by CMS/CSA is likely to be very persuasive on any court considering what is the appropriate level of maintenance [4].

Prior to 2003[5] an RP/PwC was prohibited from making an application for child maintenance if there was a pre-existing maintenance order (although this prohibition could be overridden if the RP/PwC was in receipt of benefit). Since 2003 the existence of a child maintenance order

---

[4] TW (Children), Re [2015] EWHC 3054 (Fam) [2015] 7 WLUK 806 [2016] 2 F.L.R. 1386 [2016] Fam. Law 15 referencing GW v RW (Financial Provision: Departure from Equality) [2003] EWHC 611 (Fam), [2003] 2 F.L.R. 108, [2003] 3 WLUK 500.

[5] The relevant date is 5 April 2003

only operates as a barrier to an application if it has been in force for less than 12 months[6]. Once the order has been in force for more than 12 months CMS/CSA gains the authority to make a maintenance calculation. (Some enterprising practitioners have sought to prevent CMS/CSA having jurisdiction by making a series of follow-on orders, each lasting less than 12 months or by making a series of lump-sum payment orders. In that such schemes would appear to fly in the face of the spirit of the legislation there is at least some risk that they could be overturned in favour of the legislative provisions.)

6 Section 4.10 of the Act.

CHAPTER TWO

PATERNITY

It is by no means unusual for PP/NRPs who do not have a relationship with their children (or perhaps that should be alleged children) to dispute parentage when asked by CMS/CSA to start to pay maintenance. The catalyst for such a claim of non-parentage is often an application for a liability order by CMS/CSA. So, it makes sense for practitioners to be aware of the circumstances giving rise to a determination of parentage as part of the process of making the maintenance calculation.

The relevant statutory provision is section 26 of the Act. This provides that when there is a denial of parentage the maintenance calculation shall not be made on an assumption of parentage unless specific criteria apply. These criteria are:

Case A1

- the child is habitually resident in England and Wales;
- the Secretary of State is satisfied that the alleged parent is a man who was married to, or was the civil partner of, the child's mother at some time in the period beginning with the conception and ending with the birth of the child and;
- the child has not been adopted.

Case A2

- the child is habitually resident in England and Wales;
- the alleged parent has been registered as the father of the child; and

- the child has not been adopted

Case A3

- where the result of a scientific test would be relevant to determining the child parentage and the alleged parent a) refuses to take such a test; or b) has submitted such a test and it shows there is no reasonable doubt that the alleged parent is the parent of the child.

Case A

- where the alleged parent is a parent of the child by virtue of having adopted them.

Case B

- the alleged parent is the parent of the child by virtue of an order under section 30 of the Human Fertilisation and Embryology Act 1990.

Case B1

- the alleged parent is the parent of the child by virtue of an order under section 27 or 28 of the Human Fertilisation and Embryology Act 1990.

Case C

- there is a declaration that the alleged parent is the parent of the child pursuant to sections 55A and 56 of the Family Law Act 1986 or Article 32 of the Matrimonial and Family Proceedings (Northern Ireland) Order 1989; or there is a declaration by a court in Scotland; and

- the child has not subsequently been adopted.

Case E

- the child is habitually resident in Scotland;
- the Secretary of State is satisfied that one or other of the presumption set out in section 5(1) of the Law Reform (Parent and Child) (Scotland) Act 1986 applies; and
- the child has not subsequently been adopted.

Case F

- the alleged parent has been found, or been adjudged, to be the father of the child in proceedings before any court in England and Wales for the purposes of section 12 of the Civil Evidence Act 1968 (or the equivalent Northern Irish provisions) or in affiliation proceedings before any court in the United Kingdom and that the finding or adjudication still subsists; and
- the child has not subsequently been adopted.

If the putative father was either married to or in a civil partnership with the mother or appears on the birth certificate, then parentage will be presumed, and CMS/CSA will be perfectly entitled to make a maintenance calculation. If, notwithstanding the above, the putative father wishes to dispute parentage it is then open for him to make an application to the Family Court (or High Court) for a declaration of parentage.

If the relationship between the prospective parents has not been formalised by either marriage or civil partnership then when the potential father has been contacted by CMS/CSA it is important that they immediately respond by disputing parentage, if they do not it may well be that CMS/CSA assumes that parentage is <u>not</u> being disputed and moves to make a maintenance calculation. If there is an immediate response denying paternity, then it is likely that CMS/CSA will ask one or other or both of the parties for evidence as to parentage. This usually involves DNA testing but could conceivably be other evidence, for instance the father demonstrating that they were abroad at the time of conception. If parties are asked to have a DNA test and they refuse this may well result in an adverse inference being drawn by CMS/CSA. The author is aware of cases when the mother has refused to co-operate with DNA testing and that this has resulted in CMS/CSA dropping the claim in respect of the assumed father.

Given the substantial liability that may arise from parentage there have been instances where potential fathers have sought to compromise the DNA testing process by persuading a friend or family member to impersonate them when the test is being carried out. Engaging in such activity is potentially a fraud and CMS/CSA has a group of investigators who will look into such behaviour and if the circumstances warrant it will bring criminal prosecutions against those involved. One might very well think that agreeing to pretend to be the father is a fairly foolish course of action, as it is implicit in the process that the stand-in will give a sample of their DNA, but it is perhaps evidence of the lengths that some will go to avoid liability that this happens.

If a maintenance calculation has been made it remains possible for the father to challenge paternity but it will be for them to initiate the process and to pay the fees for the testing. There is no guarantee that even if the challenge is successful that they will recover these fees. If a client wishes to engage in this process the appropriate application needs to be made to the Family / High Court. It may be that the father is not in touch with the mother and in such circumstances it can be that CMS/CSA is used as a contact address for the mother. If there is a maintenance calculation it would be prudent for the father to advise CMS/CSA of the application. Sometimes CMS/CSA may be prepared to delay enforcement/recovery actions pending the outcome of the application but there is no obligation so to do.

Applications in relation to declarations of paternity are often dealt with by lay magistrates but may be heard by district judges. At the first hearing it is customary for directions to be given for DNA testing. If there are concerns that either the mother or father may seek to manipulate the test it can be that these directions require the presence of some independent witness. The author is aware of cases where fathers have contended that while they are the parent of some of the RP/PwC's children that they are not the father of all of them. In such cases allegations have been made that the mother will arrange for a sibling to provide DNA in the place of the child whose parentage is disputed. Given that children do not generally have photo identification and that children's appearance can change quite radically even in a relatively short space of time this potentially provides a significant challenge to ensuring that proper test has been carried out.

Further complications can ensue if the "child" is a teenager and does not wish to participate in the process. Whilst a younger child will have no real ability to refuse as a child nears the age of 18 so a court is likely to place increasing weight upon their preferences in relation to the compliance with any DNA testing and it is quite possible that a court will refuse to make such an order if the teenager does not wish to be tested.

A court ordering DNA testing may well let it be known that in the event that any party were to refuse to co-operate that this might result in the court drawing what might be termed an "adverse inference" from any such refusal.

Once the DNA testing has been carried out and the results reported back to the court it will make a declaration of paternity (or non-paternity).

CHAPTER THREE

AT COURT

CPO's discretion

CMS/CSA is usually represented at court by a Court Presenting Officer ("CPO"). CPOs are not usually legally qualified, but it would be a grave mistake to underestimate their knowledge of the law and procedure in relation to child support matters. CPOs are usually civil servants, some of whom have been working for CMS/CSA for decades. The author readily acknowledges that he has learned a good deal from the CPOs he has encountered.

The CPO is not a decision-maker in relation to the quantum of child maintenance that may be outstanding, but they have a measure of discretion in respect of the cases with which they are dealing. So, if a PP/NRP attends court and provides credible information which may alter the view of CMS/CSA as to the quantum of child maintenance outstanding, or indeed whether there is a valid liability the CPO may act. In such cases it may be that the CPO will choose to adjourn a hearing pending further investigation or consideration of information and material provided by the PP/NRP.

If a PP/NRP appears to have a valid basis for disputing the claim (either as to quantum or liability or both) then it would be sensible to raise this in correspondence with CMS/CSA in advance of any hearing and to have copies of such correspondence available at the hearing. As readers will appreciate evidencing any claims or concerns is important. Parties are expected to be proactive in respect of litigation and this is all the more so in relation to CMS/CSA matters. If someone believes that they have been incorrectly assessed, then they should immediately take steps to challenge or appeal any such calculation. Simply awaiting a hearing in respect of a peripheral matter is unlikely to be terribly persuasive and given there is often an obligation to act promptly in relation to appeals and challenges any such delay may well be fatal, even if there is some merit in the matters complained of by the PP/NRP.

CMS/CSA operates and "online portal" to which PP/NRPs and RP/PwCs can upload and view documents and correspondence in relation to their case. If for some reason the portal is not operating properly then it is for the user to raise this issue and seek a resolution. Correspondence and complaints can still be made by letter.

Without wishing to be trite, someone who has a history of engagement with CMS/CSA via telephone, portal, or correspondence and has cogent evidence matters which they say are in question is likely to present a much more credible case for exercise of discretion by the CPO (and potentially the court) than someone who has refused to engage.

Making a payment

Depending on the nature of the hearing and whether or not it is accepted that some maintenance may be outstanding it may be that making a payment at court can be used to justify suspension of immediate action and get an adjournment of the hearing.

As above, credibility is important. A very good way of establishing credibility is to start to engage with CMS/CSA to discharge outstanding maintenance. CMS/CSA has the ability to take payments over the telephone and in terms of changing the dynamic from a PP/NRP being someone who is not engaging and paying to someone who is engaging and paying this can be terribly effective particularly if dealing with a lay bench.

CMS/CSA is primarily concerned with obtaining maintenance for qualifying children. While obtaining orders and findings is important, recovering payments is even more so. If money is coming in the attitude of CMS/CSA is likely to be a good deal more friendly than if there is a blank refusal to make any form of payment.

Adjournment

Most CMS/CSA cases will be listed for a first appearance amongst a whole host of other cases. Some CMS/CSA applications are routinely dealt with on bulk lists and while CMS/CSA often seek to have their matters heard by a court only dealing with their cases it is by no means unusual for them to be lumped together with other non-criminal / non-CPS matters, fare evasion, local authority education cases, RSPCA, and fishing licences are not uncommon.

This provides an opportunity for an advocate to seek an adjournment on behalf of the PP/NRP. Unless there is a substantive issue such an application will be resisted by the CPO who may well question the basis for any such adjournment. But, if the client wishes to potentially delay the day of reckoning, or genuinely has information that they think will be relevant, it may be that this is a desirable outcome. While, as readers will know only too well, there is considerable pressure within the court system to obtain a "result" rather than have a case adjourned, if it is clear that the hearing will take a significant amount of time and disrupt the ability to deal with the remainder of the court's workload it may well be that it is relatively easy to obtain the adjournment.

Potentially this would put the party at risk of costs but while there is an increasing tendency on behalf of CMS/CSA to seek its costs it remains generally the case that applications for costs are relatively few and far between. The rationale being that monies should go to paying child maintenance, (particularly if there are arrears) rather than meeting the administrative costs. As such it may be that an adjournment is a relatively risk-free option.

Avoiding a finding

Most hearings involving CMS/CSA are conducted in open court and are not in any way subject to reporting restrictions.

The author is aware that some PP/NRPs are very concerned to avoid any formal finding against them for reputational or other reasons. In general, the simplest way of avoiding a finding is to discharge any outstanding child maintenance but, of course, this is not always possible.

If it is the case that the PP/NRP is in this position, then the matters outlined above potentially provide a mechanism to avoid a substantive hearing and possible adverse finding. Of course, there are never any guarantees, but an engaged, paying (at least to some degree), and focused respondent who has provided some evidence to justify their position has by far the best chance of avoiding an immediate decision against them.

Top Tips

1. Be polite with the CPO. PP/NRPs can feel that they are being persecuted and this can breed a great deal of resentment which can carry over into interaction with the CPO. If at all possible, try and take the heat out of the situation.

2. Be patient and if acting for the PP/NRP explain what has gone wrong – CPOs are only too well aware that their organisation is far from perfect and you tend to get a lot further with a quiet word and a rye smile than you do with scorn and derision.

CHAPTER FOUR

INFORMATION OFFENCES

The Act makes provision in sections 14, 14A, 15 and 15A for the provision of information to CMS/CSA. Regulation 4 of the Child Support Information Regulations 2008/2551 sets out a comprehensive list of people who may be required to provide information to assist the Secretary of State. The provisions are potentially onerous and subject to criminal penalty in the event of non-compliance. The regulation states as follows:

4.— Information from other persons

(1) The persons listed in paragraph (2) must furnish such information or evidence as is required by the Secretary of State's and is needed—

(a) for the determination of any application made under the 1991 Act or any question arising in connection with such an application;

(b) for the making of any decision, or in connection with the imposition of any condition or requirement, under that Act; or

(c) in connection with the collection or enforcement of child support or other maintenance under that Act.

(2) The persons required to furnish information or evidence are—

(a) subject to regulation 5, the non-resident parent;

(b) a current or previous employer of the non-resident parent;

(c) a person for whom the non-resident parent is providing or has provided services under a contract for services;

(d) a person who acts or has acted as an accountant for the non-resident parent;

(e) a person, other than the applicant, who provides day to day care for a child in respect of whom an application for a maintenance calculation has been made or in respect of whom a maintenance calculation is or has been in force;

(f) a credit reference agency within the meaning given by the Consumer Credit Act 1974;

(g) a local authority in whose area the non-resident parent or the person with care resides or has resided;

(h) persons employed in the service of the Crown or otherwise in the discharge of Crown functions—

(i) under the Road Traffic (Northern Ireland) Order 1981, sections 97 to 99A of the Road Traffic Act 19882 or Part II of the Vehicle Excise and Registration Act 19943; or

(ii) under the Prison Act 1952, the Prison Act (Northern Ireland) 1953 or the Prisons (Scotland) Act 1989;

(i) a person who, in the course of business, may lawfully accept deposits in the United Kingdom;

(j) a person who, within the meaning of the Electricity Act 1989, distributes or supplies electricity;

(k) a person who is the holder of a licence under section 7 of the Gas Act 1986 to convey gas through pipes or the holder of a licence under section 7A(1) of that Act to supply gas through pipes;

(ka) a person ("P")—

(i) who is carrying on, or who has carried on, share trading or investment management;

(ii) who is communicating, or who has communicated, in the course of business, an invitation or inducement to engage in share trading or investment management;

(kb) a person (P's "intermediary") who has, or who has had, arrangements with P that P is, or was, to—

(i) carry on share trading or investment management;

(ii) communicate, in the course of business, an invitation or inducement to engage in share trading or investment management;

(kc) except where sub-paragraph (d) applies, a person providing, or who has provided, professional services to the non-resident parent, P or P's intermediary, in relation to the activities described in sub-paragraph (ka) or (kb);

(kd) a proprietor of an Academy, where "proprietor" and "Academy" have the same meaning as in section 579 of the Education Act 19966;

(l) a qualifying lender (within the meaning given in section 19(7) of the Welfare Reform and Work Act 2016);

(m) a trustee, manager or administrator of an occupational, or personal, pension scheme (within the meaning of section 1(1) of the Pension Schemes Act 19938) ;

(n) the Motor Insurers' Bureau, a company limited by guarantee, or its officers where officer has the meaning given by section 1173(1) of the Companies Act 2006.

(3) The persons mentioned in paragraph (2) (b) and (c) include persons employed in the service of the Crown or otherwise in the discharge of Crown functions.

The author would suggest that this is quite a staggering list of people and bodies who may be required to provide information to the Secretary of State. It encompasses not only the PP/NRP but also current and previous employers, local authorities, financial institutions, utilities, pension providers, credit reference agencies and accountants. There is no necessity to obtain any form of warrant to require the provision of this information, a simple letter citing the relevant legislation and potential penalties is quite sufficient.

The failure to provide information when requested is an offence punishable by a level 3 fine. There is a statutory defence for the failure to comply of "reasonable excuse". Self-incrimination does not constitute "reasonable excuse"[7]. Moreover, in considering what might constitute an excuse the defendant will have the difficulty of overcoming very strong public policy grounds requiring that absent parents pay proper maintenance for their children which will tend to require the disclosure of the information sought.

If one considers that sections 14 and 14A might be a little Draconian, then 15 and 15A are even more so. These sections provide that the Secretary of State can appoint inspectors obtain information that the Secretary of State may require in respect of any of the purposes of the Act. These purposes will include identifying potential PP/NRPs, obtaining financial information so as to make a proper maintenance calculation, identifying where a PP/NRP may be living, locating and quantifying property and assets that may be subject to enforcement action and recovery in respect of unpaid maintenance and potentially a

7 Child Maintenance and Enforcement Commission v Forrest [2010] EWHC 1264 (Admin) [2010] 5 WLUK 311, (2010) 174 J.P. 449, [2010] 2 F.L.R. 1805, [2010] 2 F.C.R. 631, [2010] A.C.D. 74, [2010] Fam. Law 911, (2010) 107(21) L.S.G. 16, [2010] C.L.Y. 1347

wide range of ancillary objectives/information. Section 15 provides as follows:

15.— Powers of inspectors.

(1) The Secretary of State may appoint, on such terms as the Secretary of State thinks fit, persons to act as inspectors under this section.

(2) The function of inspectors is to acquire information which the Secretary of State needs for any of the purposes of this Act.

(3) Every inspector is to be given a certificate of his appointment.

(4) An inspector has power, at any reasonable time and either alone or accompanied by such other persons as he thinks fit, to enter any premises which–

(a) are liable to inspection under this section; and

(b) are premises to which it is reasonable for him to require entry in order that he may exercise his functions under this section,

and may there make such examination and inquiry as he considers appropriate.

(4ZA) But the power under subsection (4) to enter any premises is exercisable only under the authority of a warrant issued under section 15A if—

(a) the premises are occupied, and

(b) an inspector has applied for admission to the premises for the purposes of exercising the power under that subsection but admission has been refused.

(4A) Premises liable to inspection under this section are those which are not used wholly as a dwelling house and which the inspector has reasonable grounds for suspecting are–

> *(a) premises at which a non-resident parent is or has been employed;*
>
> *(b) premises at which a non-resident parent carries out, or has carried out, a trade, profession, vocation or business;*
>
> *(c) premises at which there is information held by a person ("A") whom the inspector has reasonable grounds for suspecting has information about a non-resident parent acquired in the course of A's own trade, profession, vocation or business.*

(5) An inspector exercising his powers may question any person aged 18 or over whom he finds on the premises.

(6) If required to do so by an inspector exercising his powers, any such person shall furnish to the inspector all such information and documents as the inspector may reasonably require.

(7) No person shall be required under this section to answer any question or to give any evidence tending to incriminate himself or, in the case of a person who is married or is a civil partner, his or her spouse or civil partner.

(8) On applying for admission to any premises in the exercise of his powers, an inspector shall, if so required, produce his certificate.

(9) Subject to subsection (9A), if any person—

> *(a) intentionally delays or obstructs any inspector exercising his powers; or*

(b) without reasonable excuse, refuses or neglects to answer any question or furnish any information or to produce any document when required to do so under this section,

he shall be guilty of an offence and liable on summary conviction to a fine not exceeding level 3 on the standard scale.

(9A) A person is guilty of an offence under subsection (9)(a) as a result of intentionally delaying or obstructing an inspector's entry to premises that are occupied only if, at the time of the delay or obstruction, entry to the premises is authorised by a warrant issued under section 15A.

(10) In this section—

"certificate" means a certificate of appointment issued under this section;

"inspector" means an inspector appointed under this section;

"powers" means powers conferred by this section;

(11) In this section, "premises" includes–

(a) moveable structures and vehicles, vessels, aircraft and hovercraft;

(b) installations that are offshore installations for the purposes of the Mineral Workings (Offshore Installations) Act 1971; and

(c) places of all other descriptions whether or not occupied as land or otherwise,

and references in this section to the occupier of premises are to be construed, in relation to premises that are not occupied as land, as references to any person for the time being present at the place in question.

Readers will note that there is power to obtain an entry warrant to a private dwelling if required pursuant to section 15A of the Act. Notice, of 21 days, has to be given to the occupier of the premises of the application for a warrant and the application must be supported by information in writing.

The inspectors are empowered to ask questions of anybody over 18 who is at the premises and to require them to provide information and documents. If somebody at the premises intentionally delays or obstructs the inspector or, without reasonable excuse, refuses to answer questions or provide information or documents then this may be a criminal offence punishable by a level 3 fine. In contrast with the provisions of sections 14 and 14A, in respect of this section, there is protection against self-incrimination.

While still good law it seems to the author that there is a marked decrease in the use of the information gathering powers of CMS/CSA resulting in cases under these sections. This is probably because the ability to directly access HMRC records is a faster and cheaper method of getting information.

If acting for the respondent the question becomes: do they have a reasonable excuse for their action? The burden is upon them to satisfy the court that they have acted properly. Potentially an inability to identify the PP/NRP in question could be a defence. If there are two individuals with similar names and ages if may be the court could be persuaded that the correct party could not be ascertained.

It might also be possible deflect the charge if the accused can show that they were seeking clarification or further information about the target and that this had not been provided by CMS/CSA.

If the matter is to be defended then having contemporaneous documentary evidence justifying the course of action which has been taken is key to persuading the court of reasonable excuse / innocence.

In terms of mitigating any penalty the provision of the information (if somewhat belatedly) will be helpful. If done immediately on receiving the summons if may be possible to persuade CMS/CSA not to proceed with the prosecution.

Top Tips

1. Check the service of the original and any subsequent information requests.
2. Check the details of the PP/NRP that is the target of the request.
3. If possible, provide the information or evidence why it cannot be done.

CHAPTER FIVE

DEDUCTION FROM EARNINGS ORDER

A deduction from earnings order is exactly what it sounds like. It is very similar to the attachment of earnings order often used as a means of enforcement in the Magistrates' Court. It was envisaged that it would be the mainstay of recovery of unpaid maintenance.

The legislative authority for the making of Deduction from Earnings Orders ("DEO") is to be found in section 31 of the Act and in the Child Support (Collection and Enforcement) Regulations 1992/1989.

The DEO is addressed to the employer of the PP/NRP. It requires that the employer makes deduction from the wages/salary of the liable person. The order can be made to recover arrears of maintenance, amounts of maintenance which will become due in the future or a combination of the two.

The order operates as an instruction to the employer to make the applicable deduction and to pay that money to the Secretary of State.

A copy of the order is to be served upon the PP/NRP.

Again, it is worth noting the extent to which child support legislation allows CMS/CSA to require deductions direct from the liable person's salary as an administrative decision.

Section 32 of the Act makes provision for the enacting of subordinate legislation in order to implement the DEO and specifically provides a mechanism whereby the liable person can appeal to a Magistrates' Court if they are aggrieved by the order, or where there is a dispute as to whether payments constitute earnings, or any other prescribed matter in relation to the order (section 32.5).

Section 32 of the Act also contains provision that when considering an appeal the Magistrates' Court (or in Scotland the sheriff) shall not question the maintenance calculation by reference to which the DEO was made. This is a provision which is mirrored in various other areas of the Act and significantly limits the discretion and jurisdiction of the Magistrates' Court to go behind the maintenance calculation, even if on its face it was absurd.

Section 32 of the Act also creates an offence, punishable by a level 2 fine, if a person fails to comply with the order or with any regulations made pursuant to the section. There is a statutory defence that the person took all reasonable steps to comply with the relevant requirements.

Part III of the Child Support (Collection and Enforcement) Regulations 1992/1989 deals with DEOs.

Regulation 9 requires that the DEO shall specify the:

- name and address of the liable person;
- name of the employer to whom the order is directed;
- liable person's place of work, its nature, and any works or payroll number (if any of this information is known);
- liable person's national insurance number (if known);
- normal deduction rate and the date on which the order is to take effect;
- protected earnings proportion; and
- the address to which amounts deducted are to be sent.

Regulation 11 deals with "protected earnings proportion". This is a failsafe provision which ensures that the PP/NRP retains a significant proportion of their pay. It provides that any payment required to be made under a DEO is limited to 40% of the liable person's net earnings in respect of the relevant period. As readers will be aware from the Chapter 1 the maximum rate of maintenance is generally limited to 19% of the gross weekly income if there are three or more children, this is in contrast to the provisions of these regulations where the focus is not on gross weekly income but rather on net income. In practice this means that if there are arrears as well as ongoing maintenance to be recovered that someone earning, at time of writing, some £50,000 per annum would pay approximately £13,000 in tax and national insurance and then potentially be subject to a further deduction of almost £15,000. They would be paying approximately 56% of their gross income in tax, national insurance, and child maintenance, though, of course, to get to this level it would mean that there were periods when the PP/NRP had not been paying all the maintenance which was due such that an arrears balance had built up.

Other regulations deal with notifying the Secretary of State in the event that the PP/NRP no longer works for the putative employer, and the circumstances where a DEO will lapse or be discharged.

The most important regulation in respect of DEOs and the courts is regulation 22 which makes provision for an appeal.

Appeals against DEOs

Appealing against a DEO is almost always wholly pointless. This is quite a sweeping statement but as we shall see, and as is often the case in respect of child support matters, the ability to successfully challenge decisions of CMS/CSA is heavily curtailed.

Regulation 22 states as follows:

> *22.— Appeals against deduction from earnings orders*

(1) A liable person in respect of whom a deduction from earnings order has been made may appeal to the Magistrates' Court, or in Scotland the sheriff of the sheriffdom in which he resides.

(2) Subject to paragraph (2A), any appeal shall-

> *(a) where the liable person is resident in the United Kingdom, be by way of complaint for an order or, in Scotland, by way of application;*
>
> *(b) be made within 28 days of the date on which the matter appealed against arose;*
>
> *(c) where the liable person is not resident in the United Kingdom, be made within 56 days of the date on which the matter appealed against arose.*

(2A) Any appeal against a decision of the Secretary of State that the exclusion required by regulation 3(3) does not apply is—

> *(a) where the liable person is resident in the United Kingdom, to be made within 28 days of the date on which that decision is given or sent to the liable person;*
>
> *(b) where the liable person is not resident in the United Kingdom, to be made within 56 days of the date on which that decision is given or sent to the liable person.*

(3) Subject to paragraph (3A), an appeal may be made only on one or both of the following grounds-

> *(a) that the deduction from earnings order is defective;*
>
> *(b) that the payments in question do not constitute earnings.*

(3A) Where the Secretary of State is considering specifying a deduction from earnings order as a method of payment under regulation 3(1)(i)

an appeal may also be made against a decision of the Secretary of State that the exclusion required by regulation 3(3) does not apply.

(4) Subject to paragraph (5), where the court or, as the case may be, the sheriff is satisfied that the appeal should be allowed the court, or sheriff, may-

(a) quash the deduction from earnings order; or

(b) specify which, if any, of the payments in question do not constitute earnings.

(5) Where an appeal is brought on the grounds set out in paragraph (3A), and the court, or as the case may be, the sheriff, is satisfied that the appeal should be allowed the court or the sheriff is to refer the case to the Secretary of State for him to specify whichever of the methods of payment set out in regulation 3(1) he considers to be appropriate in the circumstances.

Time limits

The first thing to note in relation to a potential appeal against a DEO is the importance of making it within time. If the liable person is not resident within the UK they may have 56 days in which to lodge their appeal but generally it must be done within 28 days of the grounds on which the appeal is based arising.

It is by no means uncommon for CMS/CSA to issue a series of DEOs each replacing its predecessor. It may be that there is some typographical error or other minor mistake in the order and this is not identified when the order is issued and results in a correction which is implemented in a new DEO. This theoretically requires that the PP/NRP should make a series of appeals in respect of each of the DEOs. In practice Court Presenting Officers will often take a pragmatic view in such a situation and allow the appeal to roll over to the subsequent, effective, DEO. If this view were not to be taken it would potentially leave CMS/CSA open to a series of adverse costs orders in respect of the replaced DEOs.

Grounds/basis for appeal

There are three grounds for appealing against a DEO. Specifically:

- that the order is defective;
- that the payments and question do not constitute earnings; and
- that the Secretary of State should have concluded that it was not appropriate to use a DEO.

First ground for appeal – defective

The term "defective" is defined with in the Regulations (Reg 8). The definition is as follows:

> *"defective" means in relation to a deduction from earnings order that it does not comply with the requirements of regulations 9 to 11 and such failure to comply has made it impracticable for the employer to comply with his obligations under the Act and these Regulations;*

Regulation 9 makes provisions for the DEO to give details of the name and address of the liable person, the name of the employer, administrative details in respect of the liable person's work, the normal deduction rate and the dates on which the deductions are to be made, the protected earnings proportion and the address at which the deductions are to be sent.

Regulation 10 has been repealed.

Regulation 11 sets out what is known as the protected earnings proportion which is 60%. This means that the liable person should never receive less than 60% of their net earnings in respect of any given period.

NRP/PPs often believe that because there is some error in their address or spelling of the name that this in some way renders the DEO legally defective. Or that because they dispute the basis of the maintenance calculation or the amount of arrears that may have accrued that the Magistrates' Court as a matter of natural justice should uphold the appeal.

Unfortunately, if the DEO has resulted in monies being deducted from the PP/NRP's salary then the appeal will fail on this ground as the test has two elements both of which must be satisfied. So, the appellant must demonstrate that there is some error in the DEO **and** that this error has prevented the employer from making the deduction from the liable person's salary. If money has been deducted, and provided it leaves the PP/NRP with at least 60% of their net earnings, the employer will have complied with their obligations under the Act and Regulations.

Magistrates and District Judges sometimes question if there is any point in having this appeal right given that it is so often going to be impossible to succeed. It seems to the author that this is a very fair question and in general it is unlikely that any prejudice or inconvenience would be suffered by the PP/NRP if the employer is unable to implement the order in relation to the liable person's salary.

Second ground for appeal – not earnings

The term "earnings" is also a defined term under the regulations. Specifically, in paragraphs 3 and 4 of regulation 8. These state:

> *(3) Subject to paragraph (4), "earnings" are any sums payable to a person-*
>
> > *(a) by way of wages or salary (including any fees, bonus, commission, overtime pay or other emoluments payable in addition to wages or salary or payable under a contract of service);*

(b) by way of pension (including an annuity in respect of past service, whether or not rendered to the person paying the annuity, and including periodical payments by way of compensation for the loss, abolition or relinquishment, or diminution in the emoluments, of any office or employment);

(c) by way of statutory sick pay.

(4) "Earnings" shall not include-

(a) sums payable by any public department of the Government of Northern Ireland or of a territory outside the United Kingdom;

(b) pay or allowances payable to the liable person as a member of Her Majesty's forces other than pay or allowances payable by his employer to him as a special member of a reserve force (within the meaning of the Reserve Forces Act 1996);

(c) pension, allowances or benefit payable under any enactment relating to social security;

(d) pension or allowances payable in respect of disablement or disability;

(e) guaranteed minimum pension within the meaning of the Social Security Pensions Act 1975;

(f) working tax credit payable under section 10 of the Tax Credits Act 2002.

Very occasionally a PP/NRP may seek to make an appeal on the basis that CMS/CSA has applied a DEO to payments which they receive which they contend do not constitute earnings. This usually applies to pension payments arising on early retirement. As readers will see from the regulations above pension payments, depending on what exactly the circumstances giving rise to the payment are, fall to be treated as earnings and on occasion excluded from earnings.

The confusion and uncertainty in relation to this issue usually arises in respect of pensions payable following early retirement as the result of ill-health or disability. Employees, particularly those in the public sector, often receive relatively generous pension payments in the event that they have to retire because of some injury or illness arising as a consequence of their work. In such circumstances they not unreasonably interpret the pension as being paid in respect of disablement or disability (and so excluded from a DEO).

The one of the key cases in relation to this issue is that of *Wakefield*[8] which deals with whether particular pensions are assessable to child maintenance which is effectively the same issue as in assessing whether an income stream from a pension can be subject to a DEO. The courts have held that despite a pension being paid to someone who has retired early as a result of illness or disability this does not mean that the pension is exempt from child maintenance. It is necessary to look at the detail of the pension and consider whether it represents compensation for injury or if it is simply the payment of a pension to which the liable person has become entitled by virtue of his early retirement on ill-health grounds. On the face of it this might appear to be a distinction in search of a difference but there is a substantive issue. Specifically, if the monies paid represents direct compensation for injury, say the loss of one's arm, then this would not usually be subject to child maintenance. However, if it is simply the payment of a pension to which one is eligible because, say as the result of the loss of one's arm, one is no longer able to work, this would be subject to child maintenance.

The general principle is that income streams are subject to child maintenance (both for assessment and enforcement purposes). If the

8 Robert Stephen Wakefield v The Secretary of State for Social Security v Janet Elizabeth Foster-Wakefield SSTRF 1999/0208/C 2000 WL 440

stream is direct compensation for an injury then this is compensating the recipient for the damage (injury) that they have suffered. If the pension is simply a replacement of the earnings the injured party would have had had they been able to continue to work then it is an assessable income stream.

Pensions often contain elements of direct compensation and replacement income. In such situations CMS/CSA can require the provision of information by the pension provider quantifying the respective compensation and income elements of the payment. If for some reason CMS/CSA were to incorrectly include the compensation element then this may be a valid ground for appeal both in respect of the maintenance calculation based on the compensatory element of the pension and any enforcement action drawing on the compensation.

As noted above any tribunal considering an appeal against a DEO is specifically prohibited from questioning or challenging the underlying maintenance calculation. This could give rise to a "Catch 22" situation wherein the maintenance calculation includes the compensation and although the compensation should not be included within the calculation (or the enforcement action) it cannot be challenged. If there is a genuine risk that a compensatory element of the pension has been targeted this should be brought to the attention of the CPO and it would be sensible to have a short adjournment of the appeal to allow CMS/CSA to check the position and hopefully adjust or withdraw the DEO. It is also to be hoped that an appeal has been made against any potentially erroneous maintenance calculation which has been made. Failing this the only option might be to try Judicial Review of a decision refusing to accept the PP/NRP's evidence of the erroneous calculation.

Third ground for appeal – incorrect decision to use DEO

Amidst all the double negatives in relation to this ground of appeal there is a fairly simple if reasonably unlikely or rare issue. The ground of appeal identified in Reg 22.3A refers back to the decision of the Secretary of

State that it is appropriate to use a DEO referenced in Reg 3.3, Reg 3.4 Reg 3.5 and Reg 3.6. These state as follows:

> *(3) Where the Secretary of State is considering specifying a deduction from earnings order by virtue of paragraph (1)(i), that method of payment is not to be used in any case where there is good reason not to use it.*
>
> *(4) For the purposes of paragraph (3) the matters which are to be taken into account in determining whether there is good reason not to use that method of payment are whether the making of a deduction from earnings order is likely to result in the disclosure of the parentage of a child and the impact of that disclosure on—*
>
> > *(a) the liable person's employment;*
> >
> > *(b) any relationship between the liable person and a third party.*
>
> *(5) For the purposes of paragraph (3) the circumstances in which good reason not to use that method of payment is to be regarded as existing are—*
>
> > *(a) a member of the liable person's or parent with care's family is employed by the same relevant employer as the liable person;*
> >
> > *(b) that family member's employment requires knowledge of the relevant employer's functions in giving effect to the deduction from earnings order; and*
> >
> > *(c) as a consequence of these circumstances the liable person's employment status or family relationships may be adversely affected by the use of a deduction from earnings order as a method of payment.*
>
> *(6) For the purposes of paragraph (3) the matters which are not to be taken into account in determining whether there is good reason not to use that method of payment are—*

> *(a) the liable person's preference for a different method of payment;*
>
> *(b) the liable person's preference for a relevant employer not to be informed about that parent's maintenance liability, that parent's liability to pay a fee or the amount of a fee payable by that parent;*
>
> *(c) that a third party would become aware of the liable person's maintenance liability, that parent's liability to pay a fee or the amount of a fee payable by that parent,*
>
> *unless they are relevant to any matter falling within paragraph (4) or circumstance falling within paragraph (5).*

The mischief which the above provisions are designed to cure is a situation where liable person is working in an environment where if it was to be known that they were the father of a child it might cause them some difficulty possibly precipitating the loss of one's employment. In our modern environment and with various employment rights and protections it is quite difficult to foresee circumstances where this would give rise to a real issue, although possibly in a family-owned business where the liable person was working for their mother-in-law and notice of a DEO in relation to an unknown child came to light this could be a reason not to impose a DEO. In practice it is difficult to see how the correspondence in relation to the implementation and appeal of the DEO would not come to light, rather undermining the usefulness of the potential protection. In most cases, of course, the issue is wholly moot as the PP/NLP will be working for an organisation which has little or no interest in his domestic arrangements.

What happens if the appeal is successful?

The relevant statutory provision is Reg 22.4 set out above.

This provides that the court can quash an order or identify what income received by the liable person constitutes "earnings". If there were to be a successful appeal in relation to ground 3A then the court can refer the matter back to the Secretary of State for him to choose alternative methods of collecting child maintenance.

The court does not have the power to order that any monies collected under the DEO be returned to the liable person. It may be that CMS/CSA refund what would have been found to have been improper deductions but there is no obligation so to do and it is quite possible that, if there are arrears of child maintenance, CMS/CSA will simply retain the funds to reduce the debt.

So, unless some very unusual circumstances apply, if a DEO has successfully resulted in a deduction from a PP/NRP's wages it is most unlikely that an appeal would have any merit.

Top Tips

1. Check whether money has been paid over to CMS/CSA from the employer – if so there is little chance of there being a successful appeal on the grounds of defect.

2. If the appeal is based on the "not earnings" ground obtain evidence of the nature of the payment stream being targeted. Ask for a mandatory reconsideration and consider an immediate appeal to the First Tier Tribunal (even if the mandatory reconsideration process has not been completed.

3. Depending on for whom you are acting consider the opposition view of the payments being targeted and how you evidence the contrary position.

4. In an earnings case be wary of seeking to use the prohibition against questioning the maintenance calculation as the key defence to an appeal. The Court has the power to designate whether or not the payments in question are "earnings" so it must be entitled to query the calculation to some degree.

CHAPTER SIX

REGULAR AND LUMP SUM DEDUCTION ORDERS

Introduction

Deduction Orders ("DO") were introduced as part of a major reform of the child support legislation in 2008. There are two sorts of order, a Regular Deduction Order ("RDO") and a Lump Sum Deduction Order ("LSDO").

The legislative provisions for these orders are section 32A to 32L of the Act and regulations 25A – 25AE of the Child Support (Collection and Enforcement) Regulations 1992 (regulations 25B to 25L deal with RDOs, regulations 25M to 25W deal with LSDO and regulations 25X to 25AE apply to both).

The orders are pretty much what they sound like. The RDO allows CMS/CSA to order a financial institution to make a regular deduction from an account operated by the PP/NRP. In some ways the order is very similar to that of a deduction from earnings order but is geared towards a financial institution rather than an employer. Some liable people who are self-employed or have private income from investments or other income generating assets (properties, royalties and the like) will receive funds on a regular basis and these can be targeted by an RDO.

The LSDO is effectively a one off RDO. CMS/CSA either as a result of the use of its investigatory powers or as a result of information received from the RP/PwC may be made aware of an account operated by the PP/NRP in which there are funds which can potentially be used to discharge unpaid maintenance.

Both orders are geared to deal with arrears of maintenance and the RDO can operate to recover maintenance which will become payable at a future date as well. It is possible to make orders under this section even if there is an appeal outstanding in relation to the underlying maintenance calculation if the Secretary of State forms the view that even if the appeal were to be successful the funds recovered by the deduction order would not be affected or that it would be fair in all the circumstances to proceed.

These orders are further examples of just how far-reaching are the powers of CMS/CSA as a result of the changes to legislation implemented since 1991. CMS/CSA now has an administrative power to deduct monies from the PP/NRP's bank account. It used to be the case that DOs could not be made in relation to joint accounts such that if a PP/NRP wished to shield monies in an account from a DO this could be done by having a stooge be a joint holder of the account. Legislative changes in 2018 now means that it is possible for a joint account to be targeted.

In the event that a joint account is targeted for a DO the joint holder(s) may apply to the Secretary of State for the order to be reviewed, allowing it to be varied, or making provision for it to lapse, or be discharged.

Procedure

As noted above the process for making DOs is, in its initial stages, administrative.

For a RO the Secretary of State sends a copy of the order to the deposit taker, and this then obliges the deposit taker to make the appropriate deductions and pay the money over to the Secretary of State within seven days of receipt of the order.

The order needs to identify the account to which it applies and be directed to the deposit taker and identify the date on which it comes into effect[9]. The order operates as an instruction to make the identified

[9] S32A

deductions from the account and pay the money over. The Secretary of State is obliged to serve a copy of the order on the deposit taker, the person against whom it is made, and, if there is a joint holder of the account, on them as well.

There is an additional obligation in respect of jointly held accounts wherein the Secretary of State is obliged to offer any joint holders of the account an opportunity to make representations about the proposed RDO and any amounts due to be deducted[10]. The Secretary of State is obliged to consider whether any proposed deduction is "fair in all the circumstances" and in making this determination shall have particular regard to any representations made from any of the joint holders and the amount contributed to the account by each of them.

The procedure in relation to LSDOs is a little more complex.

The first step is that the Secretary of State makes an interim order addressed to the deposit taker or third party in question, it specifies the account in respect of which it is being made and identifies the amount of arrears of child support maintenance in respect of which the Secretary of State proposes to make the order[11]. As with an RDO the interim order must be served on the deposit taker, the liable person and any joint account holder.

If the interim order is made in respect of a joint account then it must be accompanied by a notice giving additional information[12]: the name of the liable person; that the Secretary of State has made an interim order in respect of the account and is proposing to make a final order; that the interim/final order will operate as an instruction to the deposit taker to freeze the funds in the account so that there are sufficient funds available to satisfy the order; that the interim order has been made because the

10 S32B

11 S32E

12 Reg 25MA

liable person is required to pay arrears of child support maintenance; the earliest date proposed by the Secretary of State that the funds be paid under any final order that may be made; that the account holder(s) may make representations about the proposed final order; that the final order is likely to be made in equivalent terms to the interim order if no representations are made; and the period in which representations can be made. No final order is to be made until the period for making representations has expired and that the Secretary of State has considered any such representations.

As will be gathered from the above the making of the interim order operates as a freezing order in respect of the funds in the account up to the amount sought under the interim order[13]. This freezing order operates from the service of the interim order on the deposit taker and continues until the end of the period for the making of any appeal or, if an appeal is lodged any proceedings in respect of the appeal have been concluded.

The freezing and payment provisions may be dis-applied, with the consent of the Secretary of State, in the event that any of the following apply[14]:

- the liable person, their partner, any relevant other child is suffering hardship meeting ordinary living expenses;

- another account holder, another account holder's partner or a child in relation to whom another account holder is a person with care, is suffering hardship meeting ordinary living expenses;

[13] S32G

[14] Reg 25N

- the deposit taker has a right of set-off and they satisfy the Secretary of State of an intention to exercise the right was formed in the 30 days leading up to the making of the order;

- the deposit taker and either the liable person or another account holder had made a written agreement that money standing to the credit of the account was required as security for that agreement; or

- there are any other circumstances which the Secretary of State considers justifies the release of funds / freezing provisions.

In considering the above the Secretary of State must take into account any adverse impact the decision may have on the liable person or any other person and any alternative arrangements which could be made by the liable person, any other account holder or the deposit taker.

If the liable person has no beneficial interest in any of the amount standing to the credit of the account holder(s) , then those amounts are to be disregarded.[15]

Practitioners will appreciate that if a liable person wishes to evade the impact of a RDO it is likely to be a relatively simple matter to divert any income stream away from the targeted account to an account at a new deposit taker/institution. It is likely that the costs of preparing, lodging, and trying any appeal are likely to be disproportionate to sums that might be recovered if the appeal were to be allowed.

However, in relation to LSDOs, the position can be rather different as it is not uncommon for many tens of thousands of pounds to potentially be subject to such an order. In such cases the cost benefit analysis in respect of litigating is rather different.

---

15 Reg 25Y

Role for the Courts

Regulation 25AB provides that there is a right of appeal to the Family Court/Sheriff in respect of the making of a RDO or a Final LSDO. The PP/NRP is able to make an appeal as well as any other person affected by the making of the making of the order, in practice this means joint account holders but the wording in the regulation is quite wide and could conceivably include other interested parties.

The relevant procedural rules in respect of deduction order appeals are to be found in practice direction 30A of the Family Procedure Rules 2010 starting at paragraph 9.13. There are a number of features of these rules which are quite harsh. For instance:

> *9.19 Rule 4.1(3)(a) (court's power to extend or shorten the time for compliance with a rule, practice direction or court order) does not apply to an appeal against the making of a lump sum deduction order under section 32F of the 1991 Act in so far as that rule gives the court power to extend the time set out in paragraph 9.17 for filing and serving an appellant's notice after the time for filing and serving the that notice set out in paragraph 9.17 has expired.*

The effect of this rule would appear to be that regardless of the reason for any failure to serve notice of appeal within the statutory time limit the court has no power to extend the limit. It could be that a PP/NRP receives notice of a Final Order and on the same day is on his way to the court to file the relevant notice of appeal when he is injured in an accident and rendered unconscious for the next 21 days only for the court not to be able to extend his time for appeal. Similarly, as paragraphs 9.17 and 9.18 provide that the relevant time period starts when the order is served and that this is deemed to be two days after it has been posted by CMS/CSA it would not matter if it could be demonstrated that there were no postal deliveries to the PP/NRP's address until after the deadline had expired, again the court would have no power to extend the deadline.

It is conceivable that if the situations outlined above were to take place that it might be possible to make some form of judicial review or human rights argument to say that the rules were inherently unreasonable or undermined a right to a fair trial but given that the wording of these paragraphs of the Family Procedure Rules is as explicit as it is such applications may be very difficult to win. Accordingly, in respect of any deduction order appeals it is vitally important that the relevant appeal and the associated supporting documents are filed promptly.

Paragraph 9.24 of the Rules is similarly harsh in that it removes the court's discretion to allow a variation of time limit for filing an appellant's notice late.

The test for granting an appeal in respect of a deduction order is set out in PD30.12 of the Family Procedure Rules 2010 as amended by paragraph 9.30 of PD30A. This now states:

> *(3) The appeal court will allow an appeal where the decision of the lower court or, in a deduction order appeal, the order or decision of the Secretary of State was –*
>
> > *(a) wrong; or*
> >
> > *(b) unjust because of a serious procedural or other irregularity in –*
> >
> > > *(i) the proceedings in the lower court; or*
> > >
> > > *(ii) the making of an order or decision by the Secretary of State.*

There is no definition as to what constitutes something being "*wrong*". Nor is there any definition as to what constitutes "*a serious procedural, or other irregularity*".

It would appear from the wording of the provision that it would be possible for a decision by the Secretary of State to be unjust but, if not the consequence of a serious procedural or other irregularity, then the test for granting the appeal would not be satisfied.

In practice the outcome is that judges hearing such appeals will look to see whether there is any injustice in upholding the deduction order. When exercising appeal rights most PP/NRPs will seek to raise as grounds for granting the appeal any and every issue or grievance which they may have in respect of CMS/CSA. It is also quite common for the liable person to suggest that the RP/PwC has in some way prevented from seeing the qualifying children. (Most courts will not entertain arguments in relation to access to the qualifying children without any submissions needing to be made by CMS/CSA.)

The position in respect of other arguments/grievances depends a good deal on the judge. Most judges are very active, unsurprisingly, in seeking to promote the interests of the child and the RP/PwC, however there are some occasions when the judges may become concerned about the conduct of CMS/CSA and effectively require CMS/CSA to justify their conduct of the case. Given the lack of prescription as to what constitutes being "wrong" or "unjust" the widest scope for such argument often comes in deduction order appeals.

A practitioner, dealing with such an appeal in court, needs to be aware of the provisions of s32.J of the Act, in particular 32.J.6 which states:

> *"(6) On an appeal under regulations under subsection (5), the court shall not question the maintenance calculation by reference to which the order under section 32F was made."*

This is the usual provision prohibiting the court from questioning the maintenance calculation giving rise to the liability. The extent of this prohibition will be considered below in the chapter in relation to liability orders but it is a wide-ranging bar from any challenge to the maintenance calculation and should operate to prevent arguments being raised in respect of the following, non-exhaustive, list of issues:

- the level of the income assessed in relation to the PP/NRP;
- the correctness of any deductions;
- the level of any shared care; and
- any variation or supersession resulting in a higher level of assessed income.

It is sometimes contended by the liable person that they have made payments directly to the RP/PwC or the QC(s) and so that it is wrong for CMS/CSA to be seeking to recover monies by the deduction order because these have already been paid over. If the case is a "Collect and Pay", then all maintenance payments should have been made to CMS/CSA. The relevant letters notifying the liable person of their liability make it clear that monies are to be paid to CMS/CSA. If, for whatever reason, the liable person has chosen to make payments by some other route then, if these are not accepted as maintenance by the RP/PwC, it is most unlikely that they will be accepted as such by CMS/CSA. (S32A.9 and S32E.9 of the Act specifically provide in relation to RDOs and LSDOs that unless money has been paid as directed it will not count as child support maintenance.)

The author is aware of some instances where PP/NRP's have opened bank accounts, apparently in the name of the QC or the RP/PwC into which they transfer money apparently in satisfaction of a maintenance liability. When these have been investigated it turns out that the account is controlled by the PP/NRP. It is a matter for practitioners as to how they react to being instructed that an account has been opened for the QC or the RP/PwC. Payments to the QC will not constitute a discharge of the maintenance liability as the liable person will have been directed to pay either CMS/CSA or the RP/PwC and there are no circumstances where a payment to the QC would discharge this obligation. If it is the case that it is argued that payments have been made direct to the RP/PwC and yet this is not being accepted by CMS/CSA it might be prudent to have a robust conversation with the client (or their representative as appropriate) reminding them that CMS/CSA have the ability to obtain relevant information directly from a wide range of financial institutions and is the client sure that he wishes to provoke such an investigation?

While the legislation operates to close off a good many avenues of appeal there are still issues that can be taken in relation to both RDOs and LSDOs.

In relation to a RDO Regulation 25C of the Child Support (Collection and Enforcement) Regulations 1992 provides as follows:

> *25C.— Maximum deduction rate*
>
> *(1) The deduction rate under a regular deduction order in respect of any deduction period—*
>
> > *(a) is not to exceed 40% of the liable person's gross weekly income as calculated—*
> >
> > > *(i) at the date of the current maintenance calculation, or*
> > >
> > > *(ii) where a maintenance calculation has been in force and there are arrears of child support maintenance, at the date of the most recent previous maintenance calculation; or*
> >
> > *(b) where a default maintenance decision has been made, is not to exceed £80 per week.*
>
> *(2) In this Chapter "previous maintenance calculation" means a maintenance calculation which is no longer in force.*

So, a challenge can be made in the event that more than 40% of the liable person's gross weekly income is being made subject to the RDO or, in the event that there is a default maintenance calculation, the order is for more than £80 per week.

Regulation 25D of the Child Support (Collection and Enforcement) Regulations 1992 provides as follows:

> *25D.— Minimum amount*
>
> *(1) A deduction must not be made where the amount standing to the credit of the account specified in the regular deduction order is below the minimum amount on the date a deduction is due to be made.*
>
> *(2) The minimum amount (for the purposes of this Chapter) is, where the deduction period is—*
>
> > *(a) monthly, £40;*
> >
> > *(b) weekly, £10; or*
> >
> > *(c) for any other period, £10 for each whole week in that period plus £1 for each additional day in that period,*
>
> *plus the amount of administrative costs authorised by regulation 25Z(a) (administrative costs).*

In theory the above regulation might give grounds for an appeal and certainly any CMS/CSA calculations / deductions should be considered in relation to the above criteria but in practice it is unlikely that someone with resources below the minimum amount would be in a position to fund a challenge to any RDO[16].

Regulation 25G provides that the liable person or any joint account holder with them potentially has the right to apply to the Secretary of State for a review of any RDO. In respect of such an application it is a

---

16 This is not a comment about the propriety of any such appeal, and if acting for CMS/CSA one should check that the provision is not being breached, it is merely referencing the likelihood on an appeal being made in such circumstances.

condition of being entitled to apply for the review that one of the criteria in regulation 25G.2 is satisfied, these are:

- the liable person or joint account holder satisfies the Secretary of State that some or all of the funds in the targeted account are not subject to a beneficial interest in favour of the liable person;
- there has been a change in the amount of the maintenance calculation in question;
- any amounts payable under the order have been paid;
- since the maximum deduction rate was calculated there has been a change in the liable person's income;
- due to an official error an incorrect amount has been specified in the order;
- the order does not comply with S32A.5 or regulation 25B.1 or 25C, which require that the order identify the amount in respect of which it is being made, be directed to the deposit taker at which the account is held, set out the date at which it shall become effective, detail the amounts of the deduction and the dates on which the deductions should be made, and set out the maximum deduction rate;
- in respect of a jointly held account another account holder satisfies the Secretary of State that the amount contributed to the account by the liable person and specified in the order has decreased or will decrease within the next three months; or
- in respect of a jointly held account another account holder who did not make representations pursuant to the procedure in regulation 25A1.5, 25IA.3 or 25KA.3 satisfies the Secretary of State that they had a reasonable excuse for not making

representations within the specified period and applies for a review of the order within three months of the expiry of the period for making representations.

This regulation allows interested parties to make representations to the Secretary of State as to whether or not the RDO should continue in the initial form or be revised or extinguished. If the interested party is unhappy with the decision, then they are able to use the appeal process.

Practitioners will appreciate from the above that given the relative complexity of some of the procedures necessary to implement and RDO this may give rise to error or mistake which could be successfully appealed. If dealing with such a case it would be prudent to review the calculation of the RDO to see if it has been performed correctly. If the proposed deduction falls within the relevant statutory provisions then for any appeal to be successful it will be necessary to demonstrate that something else has gone wrong. Arguments about the beneficial ownership of funds within accounts are often cited as the basis for an appeal. Obviously in such circumstances the quality of the evidence produced by the appellant will be significant, and if it is possible to obtain documentary evidence / corroboration which predates the making of the order, this may well be persuasive.

In respect of an LSDO there is the opportunity to make representations to the Secretary of State prior to the making of a final order. If a practitioner is instructed to deal with such representations it is imperative that they comply with the relevant time limits.

If it is decided to appeal either a RDO or a LSDO then the appellants notice must be filed within 21 days of the triggering event which for a liable person will usually be deemed receipt of the order or notification of the decision[17]. It should be noted that the date of the deemed receipt of the order is not necessarily the date on which the order was actually

[17] Para 9.17.

received. Para 9.18b provides that the liable person will be treated as having received the order or notification of the decision two days after it was posted by the Secretary of State. Schedule 2 to practice direction 30A of the Family Procedure Rules 2010 provides details of the documents that should be filed and served by both the appellant and the Secretary of State

The representations to the Secretary of State effectively constitute the initial hearing and the hearing before the Family Court will be treated as a re-hearing[18].

The Secretary of State is required to provide to the court and serve on all other parties to the appeal any information and evidence relevant to the making of the decision or the order being appealed within 14 days of the receipt of the appellant's notice. A respondent to an appeal (who may not be the Secretary of State) must file a respondent's notice within 14 days of receipt of the appellant's notice if they wish the decision to be upheld for reasons other than those given by the Secretary of State.[19]

In respect of any appeal the court has the following powers:

- to affirm or set aside the order or decision;
- remit the matter to the Secretary of State for the order or decision to be reconsidered with appropriate directions;
- to refer any application or issue for determination by the Secretary of State;
- make a costs order; and

[18] Para 9.30 of practice direction 30A of the Family Procedure Rules 2010.

[19] Para 9.20-9.22

- the powers may be exercised in respect of the whole or the part of any order or decision.

There is no power to award interest.

Successful appeals

As with most things to do with CMS/CSA it is difficult to mount a successful appeal.

The quite wide-ranging wording ("*wrong*" or "*unjust because of a serious procedural or other irregularity*") provide a reasonably expansive basis for raising arguments / facts which demonstrate there has been some injustice or irregularity in the making of the DO. But even allowing for this it will be necessary to provide evidence of the mistake or injustice which has led to the making of the DO.

Mistakes can of course happen, for instance in families where several of the members have very similar names and live at the same address. Counsel is aware of instances where it has been alleged that the account subject to the DO is actually an account of a family member other than the PP/NRP.

If the application is in respect of a LSDO, the reasons for the rejection of any representations made at the interim order stage provide good evidence of what it is likely the CMS/CSA objection to allowing the appeal, and provides an opportunity for the appellant to seek to rebut or counter CMS/CSA's reasoning.

It may be possible to make something of a failure to pursue the outstanding maintenance for an extended period of time. Particularly if CMS/CSA is unable to provide a rational explanation for delays (which often span many years). The author has seen cases which have been reactivated after more than a decade and where enforcement action is then implemented and has been successful in recovering unpaid maintenance. The difficulty with such generalised appeals is even if it is accepted that there is some prejudice or inconvenience to the PP/NRP it is likely that the prejudice to the child will be deemed to be more significant and so, while the court may have a good deal of sympathy with the appellant, it will have more sympathy with the child which is not being maintained.

In making the appeal it is important to focus on the particular facts demonstrating some injustice rather than straying into generalised attacks on the conduct of CMS/CSA. A focused approach is much more likely to carry weight with the court.

Top Tips

1. Check compliance with the time limits at all stages of the Deduction order process.

2. Make representations if still in time.

3. Analyse any representation and response that have been made to identify the potential issues that have been raised and see if additional evidence can be gathered to undermine the other side's case.

4. Make appeal applications promptly and allow for potential delays. Obtain proof of delivery, within the time frame, to the court even if the court refuses to accept delivery.

5. If it is taking time to gather evidence and this might endanger making the appeal in time, make the appeal and note that further evidence is being gathered and will be presented to the court.

CHAPTER SEVEN

LIABILITY ORDERS

If maintenance is not being paid it is likely that CMS/CSA will seek a liability order in the Magistrates' Court. A liability order is a passport to various debt recovery tools and potentially the imposition of sanctions upon the liable person for the failure to pay child support.

Liability orders are governed by section 33 of the Act. This states:

33.— Liability orders.

(1) This section applies where—

(a) a person who is liable to make payments of child support maintenance ("the liable person") fails to make one or more of those payments; and

(b) it appears to the Secretary of State that—

(i) it is inappropriate to make a deduction from earnings order against him (because, for example, he is not employed); or

(ii) although such an order has been made against him, it has proved ineffective as a means of securing that payments are made in accordance with the maintenance calculation in question.

(2) The Secretary of State may apply to a Magistrates' Court or, in Scotland, to the sheriff for an order ("a liability order") against the liable person.

(3) Where the Secretary of State applies for a liability order, the Magistrates' Court or (as the case may be) sheriff shall make the order if satisfied that the payments in question have become payable by the liable person and have not been paid.

(4) On an application under subsection (2), the court or (as the case may be) the sheriff shall not question the maintenance calculation you are under which the payments of child support maintenance fell to be made.

(5) If the Secretary of State designates a liability order for the purposes of this subsection it shall be treated as a judgment entered in a county court for the purposes of section 98 of the Courts Act 2003 (register of judgments and orders etc).

(6) Where regulations have been made under section 29(3)(a)–

> *(a) the liable person fails to make a payment (for the purposes of subsection (1)(a) of this section); and*
>
> *(b) a payment is not paid (for the purposes of subsection (3)),*

unless the payment is made to, or through, the person specified in or by virtue of those regulations for the case of the liable person in question.

The Child Support (Collection and Enforcement) Regulations 1992 provide further statutory footing for the process of obtaining a liability order. The key regulations are 27 and 28 which state:

27.— Notice of intention to apply for a liability order

(1) Subject to paragraph (1A), the Secretary of State shall give the liable person at least 7 days notice of his intention to apply for a liability order under section 33(2) of the Act.

(1A) Where the liable person is not resident in the United Kingdom, the Secretary of State shall give the liable person at least 28 days notice

of his intention to apply for a liability order under section 33(2) of the Act.

(2) Such notice shall set out the amount of child support maintenance which it is claimed has become payable by the liable person and has not been paid and the amount of any interest, penalty payments, collection fees or enforcement fees which have become payable and have not been paid.

(3) Payment by the liable person of any part of the amounts referred to in paragraph (2) shall not require the giving of a further notice under paragraph (1) prior to the making of the application.

28.— Application for a liability order

(1) An application for a liability order shall be by way of complaint for an order to the Magistrates' Court.

(2) Subject to paragraph (2A), there is no period of limitation in relation to an application under paragraph (1).

(2A) An application under paragraph (1) may not be instituted in respect of an amount payment of which became due on or before 12th July 2000.

(3) A warrant shall not be issued under section 55(2) of the Magistrates' Courts Act 1980 in any proceedings under this regulation.

Making the application

The first thing to note is that regulation 27 requires that the Secretary of State "shall" give the liable person notice of his intention to apply for a liability order. The use of the word "shall" is of course prescriptive and unless the notice has been given it can be argued that the necessary preliminary step to making an application has not been satisfied and the application must fail.

The reader might conclude that this would provide a useful avenue for delaying proceedings against a liable person by arguing that they have not had the relevant notice of the liability order application. However, as may be gathered from the other rather Draconian provisions of the child support legislation, there is provision to limit the scope of any such argument. Specifically, section 1.3 of the Act states as follows:

> *(3) Where under any provision of the Act or of these Regulations-*
>
> > *(a) any document or notice is given or sent to the Secretary of State, it shall be treated as having been given or sent on the day it is received by the Secretary of State; and*
> >
> > *(b) any document or notice is given or sent to any other person, it shall, if sent by post to that person's last known or notified address, be treated as having been given or sent on the day that it is posted.*

It is interesting to note the imbalance in the section wherein the Secretary of State is not deemed to have been given notice until it is actually received by them whereas everyone else is deemed to be on notice from the date that it is posted by the Secretary of State.

So, the position is that provided the correct address has been used (and this can include a former address if the liable person has not notified CMS/CSA of a change of address) notice is deemed to be received by them on the day that it was posted. This is regardless of the fact that it will be at least a day before the recipient could ever receive it and may well be several days before it is actually received, even if the post is working reasonably well.

A further example of the strictness of the child support regime is contained in regulation 28 above. In 2006 it was determined that when it came to child maintenance limitation should not apply. This means that if a debt arose on 12 July 2000 then nothing might have happened in the intervening period it would still be perfectly proper for CMS/CSA to make an application for a liability order more than 20 years after the liability arose.

Having provided notice and having allowed the notice period to elapse CMS/CSA will arrange for the issue of a summons to court to hear the application for the liability order. There is quite a good working relationship between the court staff and Court Presenting Officers who generally handle court appearances on behalf of CMS/CSA. In most regions a number of courts have been identified as specialist courts for the handling of child support applications / business. These courts will tend to allocate a day or half day for CMS/CSA business every few weeks. It is now commonplace for there to be bulk lists for liability order applications. It is also possible that sanctions hearings (which refers to applications under section 39A, and following, of the Act for potential committal to prison, removal of driving licence or travel document in respect of the failure to pay child maintenance) will also be scheduled at the same time.

Some "advocates" for PP/NRPs have sought to claim that the use of bulk lists is in some way an abuse of process or a denial of a fair trial. While there is scope for mistakes to be made, the actual process of listing such cases in bulk, is not, of itself, problematic. If someone wished to challenge the process their case will be dealt with on its own.

The hearing

Practitioners may be familiar with the bulk lists practice from applications by local authorities for liability orders in respect of unpaid council tax, energy companies for warrants for entry, train companies with unpaid fares, and certain traffic offences.

CMS/CSA will usually be represented by a Court Presenting Officer. CPOs are not usually legally qualified but are officers of the DWP who have received special training in order to present cases in court and are authorised so to do pursuant to section 48 of the Act and thereby have a right of audience. While CPOs may lack legal qualification a practitioner would be well advised to remember that they tend to be dealing with their particular area of law, day in and day out. They are often extremely knowledgeable as to both the particulars of the sections with which they are dealing and the more general issues that may arise. It would be very foolish to underestimate them, not least because they may well be well known to the magistrates. The author has been present in court when a PP/NRP was complaining about CMS/CSA playing on popular stereotypes as reported in the press only for them to be roundly rebuked by the chair of magistrates who said that whatever the practice might be elsewhere in the country they knew that the local officers were extremely diligent and fair-minded.

The CPO will usually wish to speak to anybody attending court prior to the hearing to understand and discuss their case. If somebody has a genuine concern or issue it is likely that the CPO will be prepared to adjourn the hearing to allow evidence to be presented or representations to be made and considered by the relevant case officer. It can be difficult to speak to case officers on the telephone but CPOs may be prepared to assist if the liable person has a substantive issue.

There is really only one potential challenge which will result in the extinguishing of a liability to pay child maintenance and that is a dispute about paternity (though as we will see below there is authority suggesting that this involves questioning the maintenance calculation and so it prohibited). Other challenges are likely to reduce the debt rather than eliminate it. As such unless the CPO can be persuaded that the matter should be adjourned for further consideration, they will likely seek to obtain the liability order. If there is a child maintenance debt, and given that a liability order is being sought this would seem axiomatic, and regular maintenance is not being paid, the CPO will seek to invite the PP/NRP to start to make payments of regular maintenance and, if possible, a contribution to the arrears. While a great deal will depend on the particular factual matrix in respect of any given PP/NRP if they are in the process of making payments this can act as an inhibition upon CMS/CSA taking any enforcement action after a liability order has been granted.

In the hearing the PP/NRP will be identified and then the case will be presented by the CPO. This will usually involve some basic details about the circumstances giving rise to the involvement of CMS/CSA and how the arrears of maintenance built up. It will also explain why a liability order is being sought rather than a deduction from earnings order. The CPO will likely then go on to explain the very limited discretion that the court has in respect of the application. As will be seen below the circumstances where it would not be appropriate to make a liability order are terribly limited.

The legal test

Section 33.1 sets out the circumstances in which it is appropriate to apply for a liability order. If the PP/NRP has failed to make a single payment and the Secretary of State considers that it is inappropriate to seek a deduction from earnings order or a deduction from earnings order has been put in place there are still arrears of maintenance requiring additional debt recovery tools, then the application can be made.

Liability orders are usually used in respect of the self-employed or those who are the directors and controllers of companies for whom they work. In that a deduction from earnings order is likely to be ineffective against such individuals in the event it was to be utilised, the next course of action is to seek a liability order with a view to being able to instruct bailiffs, or seek a third party debt order or a charging order.

Section 33.3 provides that the court "shall" makes the liability order if satisfied that the payments in question have become payable by the liable person and have not been paid. Section 33.4 provides the usual prohibition that the court/sheriff shall not question the maintenance calculation under which payments of child support maintenance fell to be made.

So how are these provisions to be interpreted? This has been considered by the House of Lords in the case of *Farley*[20]. Lord Nicholls of Birkenhead gave the leading speech in the case. He said:

> *"16. To my mind the language of section 33(4), read in the context of the section as a whole, on its face admits of only one interpretation: on an application for a liability order the Magistrates' Court must proceed on the basis that the maintenance assessment in question was lawfully and properly made. The court is precluded from questioning that assessment. It is precluded from questioning any aspect of the assessment. The Magistrates' Court function is to check that the assessment relates to the defendant brought before the court and that the payments in question have become payable and have not been paid. The court is not required to receive evidence that the assessment was made pursuant to an application satisfying the prerequisites set out in sections 4 to 6.*
>
> *17. That the magistrates' function should be limited in this way is readily understandable. Quite apart from any other considerations, it would be surprising if a challenge to the jurisdiction of the Secretary of State to make a maintenance assessment could be left to such a late stage as an application for a liability order. One would expect a challenge of this nature to be made at an earlier stage. Consistently with this, one would expect to find provision elsewhere in the statute enabling such a challenge to be made at an earlier stage.*
>
> *18. ... Rather, it is part of a statutory scheme which allocates jurisdiction to determine the validity of an assessment and decide whether the defendant is a 'liable person' to a court other than the Magistrates' Court."*

and

[20] Farley (FC) v Child support Agency and another [2006] UKHL 31

> *"32. My conclusion, therefore, is that section 33(4) precludes the justices from investigating whether a maintenance assessment, or maintenance calculation in the current terminology, is a nullity. That has been the position ever since section 33 was enacted in 1991. Such an investigation is a matter to be pursued today through the statutory appeal structure…."*

The effect of this decision is to severely curtail the ability of the Magistrates' Court to consider any wider issues in relation to the maintenance calculation or the general conduct of the case. If the PP/NRP accepts that they are the father of the qualifying child then the correct person has been brought before the court. If maintenance is outstanding, and of course this is a matter determined by CMS/CSA, then the two questions identified by Lord Nicholls have been answered in the affirmative and the court "shall" grant the order.The sections of the judgement quoted in paragraph 17 and 18 above served to underline and emphasise that this strict interpretation and limitation of the court's discretion was perfectly proper and lawful.

As an aside the author would note that in his judgment Lord Nicholls references a number of matters which could be raised on appeal to the Tribunal. In the years since the decision various amendments to the Act have been implemented which significantly curtail the permissible grounds for appealing CMS/CSA decisions and it might be that were the issue to be considered today that the Court would have come to a different conclusion.

Over the years there have been a number of attempts by PP/NRP's prevent the making of a liability order against them, most have been unsuccessful.

In the case of *The Queen on the application of J*[21] the NRP who had been resident in Australia, and taken Australian citizenship together with his

[21] [2002] EWHC 950 (Admin), 2002 WL31414044

wife and children returned to the UK for an extended holiday. During the course of the holiday there was an acrimonious breakup and in due course the then CSA was asked to make a maintenance assessment. The NRP refused to engage and refused to pay maintenance, in part because the PwC was preventing him, he contended, from seeing the children. In due course an application was made for a liability order which the NRP sought to defend citing:

- that he was not habitually resident within the United Kingdom,
- that as section 4 of the Act suggests some conditionality as to whether to apply for a maintenance assessment this had to be resolved before CSA had the power to make an assessment and that it was a denial of the NRP's Article 6 right to a fair trial; and
- that the CSA's making of the maintenance assessment constituted a breach of his Article 8 right to privacy.

The High Court rejected each of these arguments. In particular in relation to the residence point it noted that the argument necessarily involved a questioning of the maintenance assessment which was prohibited by section 33 of the Act.

In the Scottish case of *Child Maintenance and Enforcement Commission, Child Support Agency v Smith*[22] the argument was made that a liability order should not be granted because the applicant had failed to give reasons as to why a deduction from earnings order was not appropriate. The Sheriff held, following *Farley*, that a consideration / review as to why the Secretary of State had determined to apply for a liability order rather than using a deduction from earnings order was beyond the scope of the court hearing the application. It was not one of the questions the court

[22] 2010 Fam. L.R. 41

was required to consider. It was perfectly lawful to grant the liability order without explanation as to why this particular option had been chosen.

In the combined cases of *The Queen on the Application of Child Support Agency v L and The Queen on the Application of Child Support Agency v B*[23] the issues of whether the PP/NRP was habitually resident abroad and whether the PP/NRP was the father of the qualifying child were raised. In both these cases points were being taken which could, if they turned out to be true, extinguish any liability for child maintenance. In both cases the liable persons still had the ability to legally challenge the underlying facts (by an appeal in respect of the maintenance calculation and by seeking a declaration of paternity) although no action had yet to be commenced by either at the time of the hearing of the appeal.

Mr Justice Underhill in rejecting the PP/NRPs' submissions applied the *Farley* test.

Lest readers come to the conclusion that it is never possible to win a case against CMS/CSA perhaps the case of *Bird v Secretary of State for Work and Pensions and another*[24] may demonstrate that are sometimes courts minded to rule in favour of the liable person. In this case the liable person had been made subject to a maintenance assessment and directed that the payment should be made to the CSA, for onward transmission to the PwC, by a money transfer system known as Transcash. In this case the PP/NRP had agreed with the RP/PwC that he would pay her share of the mortgage payments on the former family home in lieu of maintenance.

In due course CMS/CSA applied for and was granted a liability order. The debt was said to be some £4000 which represented the mortgage payments made by the PP/NRP. The liability order was granted and an appeal was lodged. In allowing the appeal the court held that the mortgage payments were being made to the RP/PwC, though not by the

23 [2008] EWHC 2193, 2008 WL 3996358

24 [2008] EWHC 3159 (Admin), [2009] P. T. S. R. (C. S.) 25

method specified by CMS/CSA. This is important as section 33.6 of the Act makes it clear that a payment will not count as child maintenance unless it paid to the party identified by CMS/CSA. Although there are regulations about how such payment should be made a failure to comply with the regulations about method of payment does not contravene section 33.6. So, if a PP/NRP is instructed to pay the RP by cheque and makes the payments in cash instead (assuming this can be evidenced) these payments would be perfectly valid for the purposes of section 33. However, if the PP/NRP is instructed to pay the RP by cheque but instead pays the cheques to the QC this would be in breach of section 33.6 and unless these payments were accepted as child maintenance by the RP they would not count as maintenance and the liability order should be made.

Section 33.6, as referenced above, is potentially very important for demonstrating that payments have been missed. It would appear that some PP/NRPs prefer to make pay maintenance direct to the RP/PwC. It is likely that there are a number of motives for this choice and in a not insignificant number of cases it would appear to be because the PP/NRP wants to retain a measure of control or power over the RP/PwC. If the PP/NRP makes all the payments then all well and good, but if the payments are not all made then it is likely that the case will be moved from Direct Pay to Collect and Pay. If the PP/NRP does not then start paying CMS/CSA as directed and instead continues to pay the RP/PwC these payments do not count towards maintenance. The wording of the section seems crystal clear,

> *(6) Where regulations have been made under section 29(3)(a)–*
>
> > *(a) the liable person fails to make a payment (for the purposes of subsection (1)(a) of this section); and*
> >
> > *(b) a payment is not paid (for the purposes of subsection (3)),*
>
> *unless the payment is made to, or through, the person specified in or by virtue of those regulations for the case of the liable person in question.*

So, the payments made direct to the RP/PwC do not count for the purposes of section 33 if at the time the PP/NRP should be paying CMS/CSA[25].

A potential challenge?

On the face of it the *Farley* decision and the decisions applying it provide a very significant hurdle to any potential challenge to the making of a liability order if it is accepted that the person summonsed to court is the correct individual and they have not made all the payments directed by CMS/CSA. However, the concluding paragraph of Lord Nicholls's judgement potentially provides an avenue for delaying the making of an order.

The relevant paragraph is 33 and this states as follows:

> *33. I add a brief postscript. The House was told that sometimes applications for liability orders are made and granted, and liability orders are enforced, even though at the time appeals against the validity of the relevant maintenance calculations are pending. Clearly there are*

---

25 The relevant regulations are the Child Support (Collection and Enforcement) Regulations 1992/1989, Reg 2:

2.— Payment of child support maintenance

(1) Where a maintenance [calculation]1 has been made under the Act and the case is one to which section 29 of the Act applies, the Secretary of State may specify that payments of child support maintenance shall be made by the liable person-

(a) to the person caring for the child or children in question or, where an application has been made under section 7 of the Act, to the child who made the application;

(b) to, or through, the Secretary of State; or

(c) to, or through, such other person as the Secretary of State may, from time to time, specify.

(2) In paragraph (1) and in the rest of this Part, "liable person" means a person liable to make payments of child support maintenance.

> *circumstances where this may be justified; for instance, where it is necessary to take steps to prevent assets from being put beyond reach. Equally clearly there may be circumstances where it would be oppressive to follow this course. I wish to note only that when faced with an application for a liability order where an appeal is pending against the validity of the underlying maintenance calculation the magistrates should consider whether it would be oppressive to make a liability order. If they consider it would be oppressive they should adjourn the hearing, pending the outcome of the appeal or for such shorter period and on such terms as may be just. The magistrates have this power under section 54 of the Magistrates' Courts Act 1980.*

Advocates for PP/NRPs often use this passage as justification for dismissing a liability order application if an appeal is pending. However, that is both to over and understate the extent of his Lordship's qualification. A number of considerations arise from this paragraph. These include:

- His Lordship's comment is *obiter dicta*, not part of the *ratio* of the decision and as such is not prescriptive.

- The question is whether the making of the liability order could be "oppressive". Oppression is not a statutorily defined term, but it is a reasonably high bar to meet. Dictionary definitions include "prolonged cruel or unjust treatment or exercise of authority". It is to be doubted whether something that is unfair or a little harsh would meet the necessary standard.

- The fact that an appeal is about to be lodged or is outstanding does not meet Lord Nicholls's threshold. For him the appeal would have to be against the validity of the relevant maintenance calculation, not simply its quantum. Effectively the appeal would need to extinguish the liability in total to potentially trigger an assertion of oppression.

- Magistrates are often told that somebody is going to make an appeal of some sort. As practitioners know parties often do not follow through in making such an application. Moreover, the ability to make an out of time appeal is often heavily restricted/curtailed in relation to child support matters.

- The court also notes that even if there is a valid appeal it may well be that it is appropriate to make the order anyway if there is a risk that assets might be put beyond the reach of CMS/CSA. This could include a situation where there is a risk that some other party could leapfrog CMS/CSA in obtaining security over the PP/NRP's assets.

- Appeals in relation to maintenance calculation can be in relation to the totality of liability but more often are going to be in respect of liability for particular periods, perhaps because the wrong level of income has been used. It is quite possible for there to be a valid ground of appeal in respect of child maintenance debt arising in part of the period covered by a liability order. While the PP/NRP may wish to have the liability order dismissed entirely this would be to go too far.

- His Lordship suggests, that if the making of the liability order might be oppressive that the appropriate course of action is not to dismiss the application but rather to adjourn it pending the outcome of the appeal or for such other period of time as they deem just.

If you are tasked with representing a liable person in respect of a liability order application it will generally be an uphill task to show that the application should be dismissed unless there has been a fairly serious error in identifying the correct liable person. However, there is some limited scope to seek an adjournment in the event that there is a pending appeal. If on reviewing the case you conclude that there may have been an error in the maintenance calculation attending court and providing evidence of the basis of the error may be sufficient to persuade the CPO that the matter should be adjourned for further examination by CMS/CSA. There is no guarantee, but a constructive conversation can usually be had. The PP/NRP's credibility can be boosted if they are making regular payments of maintenance (even if this is not all that CMS/CSA say is due).

Top tips

1. If you are acting for the PP/NRP and have been instructed prior to the hearing it may be worthwhile seeing if you can make an out of time appeal in respect of the maintenance calculation.

2. If there has been a 25% variation in the PP/NRP's income, then this can be sufficient to trigger a variation in the maintenance calculation prior to the annual review. Making representations to CMS/CSA in respect of this change of circumstances could be used as an argument to adjourn the liability order hearing. It is pretty tenuous, but it might be possible to persuade the court that it should adjourn consideration of the liability order to allow the new information to be considered and an assessment made as to whether or not it impacts the liability order period. (As noted above Lord Nicholls set quite a high threshold for any such argument but it might be that you can persuade the bench to implement a lower threshold.)

3. If the PP/NRP is claiming to have made payments to the RP/PwC then it may be possible to persuade CMS/CSA to adjourn the case while these payments are investigated. If bank statements are available showing regular payments to the RP/PwC this is obviously very helpful evidence. If there is some other evidence, receipts (it does sometimes happen), evidence of regular cash withdrawals, email, WhatsApp, text messages or the like where the RP/PwC is asking for cash from the PP/NRP and there is evidence of payment. Do bear in mind that while there may be evidence of

payments being made they may not be child maintenance – they could be loan repayments or spousal support.

4. If the PP/NRP wishes to dispute paternity and has a good back story this may be sufficient to persuade either CMS/CSA or the court that the matter should be adjourned to allow an application for a declaration of paternity. In a very extreme case the author was present in court when the PP/NRP asserted, with a good deal of credibility, that the RP/PwC had been operating as a sex worker at the time of conception of the QC. In theory the authority[26] suggesting that such an action would amount to a challenge to the maintenance calculation and so should be discounted should prevail but sometimes lay benches can be persuaded to adjourn the matter.

5. In practice in most cases the best that one can hope for as a respondent advocate is that the matter is adjourned but some lay clients would regard this as a worthwhile outcome.

---

[26] The Queen on the Application of Child Support Agency v L and The Queen on the Application of Child Support Agency v B [2008] EWHC 3159 (Admin), [2009] P. T. S. R. (C. S.) 25

CHAPTER EIGHT

SET-ASIDE APPLICATIONS

If a liability order is made against the client then it can be, and should be, appealed pursuant to section 111A of the Magistrates' Court Act 1980 this states:

"111A Appeals on ground of error of law etc in child support proceedings

(1) This section applies in relation to proceedings under the Child Support Act 1991 in a Magistrates' Court.

(2) Any person who was a party to any proceeding before the court, or is aggrieved by the order, determination or other proceeding of the court, may question the proceeding on the ground that it is wrong in law or is in excess of jurisdiction by appealing to the Family Court.

(3) But a person may not appeal under subsection (2) in respect of a decision if–

(a) the person has a right of appeal to the county court or the Family Court against the decision otherwise than under this section, or

(b) the decision is final by virtue of any enactment passed after 31st December 1879.

(4) A notice of appeal under subsection (2) shall be filed within 21 days after the day on which the decision of the Magistrates' Court was given."

Practitioners will note that the appeal must be filed within 21 days of the decision being given by the magistrates. This is a very strict deadline. The relevant rules in relation to such appeals are contained in Practice Direction 30A of the Family Procedure Rules 2010. These state:

> *"Appeals to the Family Court from decisions in child support proceedings under section 111A of the Magistrates' Courts Act 1980 ('the 1980 Act')*
>
> *[3.1205]*
>
> *9.3 Section 111A of the 1980 Act, provides that in proceedings under the Child Support Act 1991 a person may appeal to the Family Court on the ground that a decision is wrong in law or is in excess of jurisdiction. Section 111A(3)(a) provides that no appeal may be brought under section 111A if there is a right of appeal to the Family Court against the decision otherwise than under that section. Such an appeal is usually heard by a judge of circuit judge level court in accordance with the rules relating to the composition of the court and distribution of business made in accordance with section 31D of the 1984 Act.*
>
> *9.4 Subject to section 111A of the 1980 Act and any other enactment, the following rules in Part 30 apply to appeals under section 111A of the 1980 Act –*
>
> > *(a) 30.1 (scope and interpretation);*
> >
> > *(b) 30.2 (parties to comply with the practice direction);*
> >
> > *(c) 30.4 (appellant's notice);*
> >
> > *(d) 30.6 (grounds of appeal);*
> >
> > *(e) 30.8 (stay); and*
> >
> > *(f) 30.9 (amendment of appeal notice).*

> *9.5 Section 111A(4) of the 1980 Act provides that the notice of appeal must be filed within 21 days after the day on which the decision of the Magistrates' Court was given. The notice of appeal should also be served within this period of time. The time period for filing the appellant's notice in rule 30.4(2) and (3) does not apply. There can be no extension of this 21 day time limit under rule 4.1(3)(a)."*

Readers will see from the above that the court has no power to extend the deadline for filing the appeal even if the appellant has a very good reason for not making the appeal in time.

Set-aside applications

PP/NRP's often appear to exhibit a wilful desire or reckless tendency to refuse to engage with CMS/CSA. This refusal is sometimes displaced by the arrival of the notice of the liability order having been granted and / or notice that it has been lodged with the County Court. This can result in them contacting the Magistrates' Court to challenge the making of the liability order. In theory if such contact were to be received the proper course of action would be to refer the PP/NRP to the appropriate appeal route (detailed above). However, what often happens is the matter is simply listed for the court to consider whether the liability order should be set aside. Part of the reason that this course of action is adopted is because section 142 of the Magistrates' Court act 1980 provides a power for magistrates to re-open cases in the event of a mistake. The problem is that this section only applies to criminal cases. No such power exists under statute in respect of civil cases.

This might very well lead practitioners to believe that this would be the end of the matter but, as so often in the law, the position is a little more complicated. In the case of *R. (on the application of Newham LBC) v Stratford Magistrates' Court*[27] it was held that the magistrates did have a

---

[27] [2008] EWHC 125 (Admin), [2008] 1 WLUK 112, (2009) 172 J.P. 30, [2008] R.A. 108, [2009] C.L.Y. 2616

common law power to reopen cases. This power is exercisable if three tests are met, these are:

- there must be a genuine and arguable dispute;
- the original decision must have been made as a consequence of a substantial procedural error defect or mishap; and
- the applicant needs to act promptly on becoming aware of the court's decision.

As to what constitutes "promptly" there is no specific guidance, and it is possible that even if there has been a passage of more than a year since the decision the applicant may be able to demonstrate that they have acted promptly. The longer the passage of time the better the evidence justifying the delay will need to be. This is particularly so given the strictness of the deadline set under the formal appeal procedure. There is an inherent imbalance if the common law process allows a longer time to make the appeal than the statutory process.

What constitutes a substantial procedural error, defect or mishap is also a matter for the evidence in support of the application. It has been argued that the failure to receive notice of the hearing is sufficient to satisfy this requirement. Much will depend upon the facts, and as practitioners know hearings may often proceed when the respondent has not received notice if the notice has nevertheless been validly and properly served.

The final element that must be demonstrated is that there is a genuine and arguable dispute. As readers will have seen from the previous chapter it is very difficult for there to be a proper basis to challenge the making of the liability order if the correct person has been targeted and not all the maintenance payments have been made.

Generally, CMS/CSA will not seek costs in relation to an initial hearing where the matter has been listed by the court to consider a set-aside. If one is acting for a PP/NRP in such a situation, (it is not unusual for them to make the application themselves, usually by letter, but to seek legal advice as the hearing draws near) it should be fairly obvious whether this is one of the rare cases when there has been a mistake as to identity or some other substantive defect in making the maintenance calculation which might be sufficient to make CMS/CSA wish to review the case before seeking the liability order. In the likely event that there is no genuine and arguable dispute it may be that the best result which can be hoped for by the client is that they are able to extricate themselves from the proceedings without a costs order against them.

Unfortunately, some PP/NRP's are determined to have their day in court. It is likely that the Court Presenting Officer will try and persuade the magistrates to immediately dismiss the application rather than incur further costs in what is likely to be a futile hearing. In order to rebut such an application it would be necessary to demonstrate how the three tests identified above could be evidenced and so justify a substantive hearing.

If the matter is adjourned for a substantive hearing the court may give directions as to the evidence that it wishes to see. In that liability order hearings are largely administrative, not evidential, even if the PP/NRP believes they have suffered an injustice as a result of the maintenance calculation as we have already noted, this something which is expressly removed from the magistrates' consideration. Any directions requiring the provision of information by CMS/CSA are likely to be seen as being a collateral attack on the statutory provision, as explained by the House of Lords, taking consideration of the maintenance calculation away from the magistrates.

If faced with such a situation it would probably be prudent to write to the client warning them of the weakness of their case and the risk of costs.

Top Tips

1. Identify, how promptly the application has been made and what, if any, evidence there is to justify the delay.

2. Consider what might constitute a significant procedural error / defect / mishap.
3. Determine whether there is any basis to challenge the making of the liability order or for the adjournment of the hearing.

CHAPTER NINE

SANCTIONS

As has been noted there are a wide range of personality types who may be the subject of the maintenance calculation and enforcement activities of CMS/CSA. Some are deeply chaotic individuals who lack the ability to hold down regular employment and make regular payments of their maintenance. Others may wish to make the appropriate contribution for the welfare of their children but as a result of unfortunate circumstances are unable to do so and fall behind in their obligations. A typical case fulfilling this category might be someone involved in a serious car accident or subject to a severe illness. The third category are those who are determined not to hand over child maintenance whatever the circumstance.

If it has not been possible to recover the maintenance owed using its other enforcement / collection powers then CMS/CSA may take steps to summon the PP/NRP to court and invite the court to apply one of the sanctions provisions available under the Act.

At time of writing the three sanctions available are:

- committal to prison for a period of up to 42 days;
- removal of driving licence for up to 2 years; or
- removal of passport or travel authorisation for up to 2 years.

The sanctions may soon be supplemented by provisions allowing curfew/tagging of PP/NRPs.

The imposition of a sanction is a punishment for the failure to pay child maintenance it is not an alternative to the payment. The obligation to make the payment remains and if the debt is not paid after the expiry of the period of the punishment CMS/CSA may well institute further sanctions proceedings.

The relevant statutory provisions are sections 39A & 39B and 40 & 40B. These provide as follows:

> *39A.— Commitment to prison and disqualification from driving.*
>
> *(1) Where the Secretary of State has sought–*
>
> > *(a) in England and Wales to recover an amount by virtue of section 35(1) ; or*
> >
> > *(b) to recover an amount by virtue of section 36 or 38,*
>
> *and that amount, or any portion of it, remains unpaid the Secretary of State may apply to the court under this section.*
>
> *(2) An application under this section is for whichever the court considers appropriate in all the circumstances of–*
>
> > *(a) the issue of a warrant committing the liable person to prison; or*
> >
> > *(b) an order for him to be disqualified from holding or obtaining a driving licence.*
>
> *(3) On any such application the court shall (in the presence of the liable person) inquire as to–*
>
> > *(a) whether he needs a driving licence to earn his living;*
> >
> > *(b) his means; and*
> >
> > *(c) whether there has been wilful refusal or culpable neglect on his part.*

(4) The Secretary of State may make representations to the court as to whether the Secretary of State thinks it more appropriate to commit the liable person to prison or to disqualify him from holding or obtaining a driving licence; and the liable person may reply to those representations.

(5) In this section and section 40B, "driving licence" means a licence to drive a motor vehicle granted under Part III of the Road Traffic Act 1988.

(6) In this section "the court" means–

> *(a) in England and Wales, a Magistrates' Court;*
>
> *(b) …*

39B Disqualification for holding or obtaining United Kingdom passport.

(1) The Secretary of State may apply to the court for an order under this section against a person where—

> *(a) Secretary of State has sought to recover an amount from the person by means of taking enforcement action by virtue of section 35 or 38, or by means of a third party debt order or a charging order by virtue of section 36;*
>
> *(b) the whole or any part of the amount remains unpaid; and*
>
> *(c) the Secretary of State is of the opinion that there has been wilful refusal or culpable neglect on the part of the person.*

(2) For the purposes of subsection (1)(a), the Secretary of State is to be taken to have sought to recover an amount by means of a charging order if an interim charging order has been made, whether or not any further steps have been taken to recover the amount.

(3) A person against whom an order under this section is made is disqualified for holding or obtaining a travel authorisation while the order has effect.

(4) On an application under subsection (1) for an order against a person the court shall (in the presence of that person) inquire as to—

(a) whether the person needs a travel authorisation to earn a living;

(b) the person's means;

(c) whether there has been wilful refusal or culpable neglect on the part of the person.

(5) If, but only if, the court is of the opinion that there has been wilful refusal or culpable neglect on the part of the person, it may make an order under this section.

(6) The court may not take action under both this section and section 40.

(7) On an application under subsection (1) the court shall not question—

(a) the liability order by reference to which the [Secretary of State]3 acted as mentioned in paragraph (a) of that subsection; or

(b) the maintenance calculation by reference to which that liability order was made.

(8) An order under this section shall specify the amount in respect of which it is made, which shall be the aggregate of—

(a) the amount sought to be recovered as mentioned in subsection (1)(a), or so much of it as remains unpaid; and

(b) an amount (determined in accordance with regulations made by the Secretary of State) in respect of the costs of the application under this section.

(9) A court which makes an order under this section shall require the person to whom it relates to produce any travel authorisation that the person holds.

(10) The court shall send to the prescribed person any travel authorisation produced to the court under subsection (9).

(11) Where a court—

(a) makes an order under this section, or

(b) allows an appeal against such an order,

it shall send notice of that fact to the Secretary of State; and the notice shall contain such particulars and be sent in such manner and to such address as the Secretary of State may determine.

(12) In this section "travel authorisation" means—

(a) a United Kingdom passport (within the meaning of the Immigration Act 1971);

(b) an ID card issued under the Identity Cards Act 2006 that records that the person to whom it has been issued is a British citizen.

(13) In this section (except for the purposes of subsection (11)(b)) and in sections 39C to 39E, "court" means—

(a) in relation to England and Wales, a Magistrates' Court;

(b) …

40.— Commitment to prison.

(3) If, but only if, the court is of the opinion that there has been wilful refusal or culpable neglect on the part of the liable person it may—

(a) issue a warrant of commitment against him; or

(b) fix a term of imprisonment and postpone the issue of the warrant until such time and on such conditions (if any) as it thinks just.

(4) Any such warrant—

(a) shall be made in respect of an amount equal to the aggregate of—

(i) the amount outstanding, as defined by paragraph 50(3) of Schedule 12 to the Tribunals, Courts and Enforcement Act 2007 (taking control of goods); and

(ii) an amount (determined in accordance with regulations made by the Secretary of State) in respect of the costs of commitment; and

(b) shall state that amount.

(5) No warrant may be issued under this section against a person who is under the age of 18.

(6) A warrant issued under this section shall order the liable person—

(a) to be imprisoned for a specified period; but

(b) to be released (unless he is in custody for some other reason) on payment of the amount stated in the warrant.

(7) The maximum period of imprisonment which may be imposed by virtue of subsection (6) shall be calculated in accordance with Schedule 4 to the Magistrates' Courts Act 1980 (maximum periods of imprisonment in default of payment) but shall not exceed six weeks.

(8) The Secretary of State may by regulations make provision for the period of imprisonment specified in any warrant issued under this section to be reduced where there is part payment of the amount in respect of which the warrant was issued.

(9) A warrant issued under this section may be directed to such person or persons as the court issuing it thinks fit.

(10) Section 80 of the Magistrates' Courts Act 1980 (application of money found on defaulter) shall apply in relation to a warrant issued under this section against a liable person as it applies in relation to the enforcement of a sum mentioned in subsection (1) of that section.

(11) The Secretary of State may by regulations make provision—

> *(a) as to the form of any warrant issued under this section;*
>
> *(b) allowing an application under this section to be renewed where no warrant is issued or term of imprisonment is fixed;*
>
> *(c) that a statement in writing to the effect that wages of any amount have been paid to the liable person during any period, purporting to be signed by or on behalf of his employer, shall be evidence of the facts stated;*
>
> *(d) that, for the purposes of enabling an inquiry to be made as to the liable person's conduct and means, a justice of the peace may issue a summons to him to appear before a Magistrates' Court and (if he does not obey) may issue a warrant for his arrest;*

(e) that for the purpose of enabling such an inquiry, a justice of the peace may issue a warrant for the liable person's arrest without issuing a summons;

(f) as to the execution of a warrant for arrest.

(12) ...

40B.— Disqualification from driving: further provision.

(1) If, but only if, the court is of the opinion that there has been wilful refusal or culpable neglect on the part of the liable person, it may–

(a) order him to be disqualified, for such period specified in the order but not exceeding two years as it thinks fit, from holding or obtaining a driving licence (a "disqualification order"); or

(b) make a disqualification order but suspend its operation until such time and on such conditions (if any) as it thinks just.

(2) The court may not take action under both section 40 and this section.

(3) A disqualification order must state the amount in respect of which it is made, which is to be the aggregate of–

(a) the amount outstanding, as defined by paragraph 50(3) of Schedule 12 to the Tribunals, Courts and Enforcement Act 2007 (taking control of goods); and

(b) an amount (determined in accordance with regulations made by the Secretary of State) in respect of the costs of the application under section 39A.

(4) A court which makes a disqualification order shall require the person to whom it relates to produce any driving licence held by him.

(5) On an application by the Secretary of State or the liable person, the court–

(a) may make an order substituting a shorter period of disqualification, or make an order revoking the disqualification order, if part of the amount referred to in subsection (3) (the "amount due") is paid to any person authorised to receive it; and

(b) must make an order revoking the disqualification order if all of the amount due is so paid.

(6) The Secretary of State may make representations to the court as to the amount which should be paid before it would be appropriate to make an order revoking the disqualification order under subsection (5)(a), and the person liable may reply to those representations.

(7) The Secretary of State may make a further application under section 39A if the amount due has not been paid in full when the period of disqualification specified in the disqualification order expires.

(8) Where a court–

(a) makes a disqualification order;

(b) makes an order under subsection (5); or

(c) allows an appeal against a disqualification order,

it shall send notice of that fact to the Secretary of State; and the notice shall contain such particulars and be sent in such manner and to such address as the Secretary of State may determine.

(9) Where a court makes a disqualification order, it shall also send any driving licence , on its being produced to the court, to the Secretary of State at such address as the Secretary of State may determine.

(10) Section 80 of the Magistrates' Courts Act 1980 (application of money found on defaulter) shall apply in relation to a disqualification order under this section in relation to a liable person as it applies in relation to the enforcement of a sum mentioned in subsection (1) of that section.

(11) The Secretary of State may by regulations make provision in relation to disqualification orders corresponding to the provision he may make under section 40(11).

(12) ...

We should observe that the provisions above allow in the early 21st-century the potential imprisonment of the PP/NRP in the event that they do not pay their child maintenance. This is committal to prison for a civil debt.

The second thing to note is that in applying an overzealous interpretation of the procedure for imposing a sanction CMS/CSA implemented a policy protocol that did not comply with the legislation and when it was challenged in the appeal court the protocol was struck down and there was a wide-ranging and expensive programme of remedial action that required the withdrawal of many cases and the removal of previously imposed sanctions. Many of these cases had to be restarted. The reader can imagine the cost both in cash and in resources that this occasioned. The case, which might be said to be one of the blackest days in CMS/CSA history was *Karoonian v Child Maintenance and Enforcement Commission*[28].

---

28 [2012] EWCA Civ 1379, [2013] P.T.S.R. 635, [2012] 10 WLUK 928, [2013] 2 Costs L.O. 187, [2013] 1 F.L.R. 1121, [2012] 3 F.C.R. 491, [2013] H.R.L.R. 3, [2013] Fam. Law 22, Times December 27, 2012, [2013] C.L.Y. 1239

As a consequence of the *Karoonian* decision CMS/CSA have amended their practices so as to address the issues raised in the judgement. This is done by taking the following steps.

1. Obtaining a liability order.

2. Inviting the PP/NRP to start to pay their child maintenance debt.

3. Seeking to enforce the liability order by Bailiff action or by seeking a charging order or third-party debt order.

4. Warning the PP/NRP of the potential enforcement / imposition of sanctions action (being an application to seek the removal of passport or driving licence or possibly committal to prison). This will usually be accompanied by a "money in/money out" form which the PP/NRP will be invited to complete. It is not unlike a means form in the Magistrates' Court. It gives the PP/NRP the opportunity to provide up-to-date information about their financial circumstances.

5. Summoning the PP/NRP to court for a sanctions hearing. The summons will usually be accompanied by a witness statement from the Court presenting Officer together with a bundle of documents which will include the liability order, evidence of enforcement by Bailiff or other action (usually a certificate of Nulla Bona), information from the Financial Investigations Unit ("FIU") which will involve an analysis of the PP/NRP's bank statements, usually for a period of six months, and will set out the money that they have received and "non-essential / discretionary" spending which could have been used to start to deal with the child support debt.

Compelling attendance at court

If the liable person does not attend court then the Court presenting Officer will likely apply for a warrant of arrest. The legal power to arrest someone in order to compel them to attend court in relation to a matter concerning civil debt arises from regulation 33 of the Child Support (Collection and Enforcement) Regulations 1992. It is a matter for the court as to whether or not the warrant is backed for the bail. Generally, if it is the first occasion that someone fails to attend court CMS/CSA would invite the court to allow bail. However, much depends on the attitude of the liable person and there are often occasions when the conduct of the PP/NRP is such that the court will be invited to issue a "no bail" warrant. If the PP/NRP has been abusive to CMS/CSA or court staff, or others or has made statements evidencing a determination not to pay child maintenance or engage with CMS/CSA these events will be described to the court and it is likely that the "no bail" warrant will be issued.

While there was a time that these warrants would be executed by the police now the position is that a private Bailiff company, usually Marstons will execute the warrant on behalf of CMS/CSA. In general bailiffs do not have a power of arrest however there are a number of individuals within these private debt collection companies who have the necessary certification to allow them to detain people. They have handcuffs.

In most cases after the issue of the warrant it will be passed to the Bailiff company and they will contact the liable person by post or phone and tell them that a warrant of arrest has been issued. Usually this is sufficient to persuade the liable person that they can no longer ignore the CMS/CSA process and that they need to attend court. They will be given a date and location for a hearing. Readers can well imagine that some PP/NRPs are sufficiently chaotic in their lives and others are so entrenched in their positions that they fail to attend court even after being advised of the warrant. In such cases the failure to attend will almost certainly result in the issuance of a "no bail" warrant.

In practice, even on a "no bail" warrant, the liable person will not face being detained overnight. (Though theoretically, it is possible). The usual practices that the Bailiff will seek to arrest the liable person early in the morning of a day when CMS/CSA already have a number of cases listed in the local Magistrates' Court. All being well he will be brought before the court and the sanctions hearing will proceed. If for some reason there is insufficient time the case may be adjourned and the PP/NRP bailed to attend on the next occasion.

Legal representation / negotiation

While in general CMS/CSA regard the imposition of a sanction rather than the recovery of maintenance as something of a failure it is axiomatic that an application for sanctions, including the potential for committal, means that there is a risk of a custodial penalty upon the liable person.

It is now accepted that given there is a risk of custody the PP/NRP should have the opportunity to obtain legal advice prior to a substantive consideration of the case[29]. In that these cases are held that the Magistrates' Court there will usually be a duty solicitor in attendance who can provide this advice. However, it is something of a moot point as to whether or not the legal aid scheme covers civil matters. Some knowledgeable duty solicitors take the view that they will not see a PP/NRP because this means that the court cannot impose a custodial sanction. Whether in practice this is actually in the client's best interests may be arguable as they might be better served by engaging with CMS/CSA and negotiating, with the benefit of the duty solicitor's assistance, a manageable payment plan.

If you are acting for CMS/CSA in such a situation you may well need to assist the duty solicitor as to the process which is about to be commenced. Hopefully the PP/NRP, will have brought a copy of the witness statement and exhibits which were served upon him. If he has not it may be that the CPO has a spare copy of the bundle or that it can be passed

[29] Douherty v Chief Constable of Essex [2019] EWCA Civ 55 [2019] 1 WLUK 264 and O (Committal: Legal Representation), Re [2019] EWCA Civ 1721, [2019] 4 W.L.R. 140, [2019] 10 WLUK 246, [2019] Costs L.R. 1559, [2020] 1 F.L.R. 288, [2020] 1 F.C.R. 258, [2020] C.L.Y. 160

to the duty solicitor by the court (who should also have received an electronic copy of the bundle prior to the hearing).

The key objective of CMS/CSA is to obtain money for the RP/PwC. They will usually be prepared to enter into a negotiation with the PP/NRP with a view to him commencing payments of child support. Their general target is to recover the arrears within two years. Sometimes this is a wholly fanciful objective given the level of arrears and the income of the PP/NRP but it is something to keep in mind in respect of any proposals to be put to CMS/CSA. CMS/CSA will usually seek to obtain a finding of wilful refusal/culpable neglect and the imposition of a penalty but postponed on agreed terms. It may be possible to negotiate an adjournment of the hearing on the basis that payments start by saying that the funding for the payments is conditional upon there being no finding against the PP/NRP.

<u>The hearing</u>

Usually CMS/CSA sanctions hearings will take place in a normal criminal courtroom with a secure dock but sometimes they are heard in family or youth courts. In the latter case the applicant's advocate should consider whether the matter should be moved to a court with secure facilities. (If one is acting for a PP/NRP and a couple of burly security guards arrive in court just before the bench returns to give their decision and reasons it is a sign that matters have not gone well for the client. Seeking instructions to make an improved offer should be canvassed urgently in such a situation.)

The way the hearing proceeds is very much in the hands of the tribunal. Usually, it will be on the basis of an agreed payment plan but this is subject to the attitude of the Court. Some District Judges take a very dim view of the failure to pay maintenance and the author has been present when PP/NRPs have refused to make offers and the Judge has invited them to reconsider their position. Such reconsideration to take place in the cells.

To assist Magistrates' Courts in dealing with sanctions cases the Justices' Clerks Society (the professional society for legal advisers in the Magistrates' Court) has produced a 29-page document entitled Enforcement of Child Maintenance Following a Liability Order: Checklists. It suggests the proper process for dealing with applications arising from section 39A of the Act.

The checklists

There are separate checklists in relation to the potential sanctions; removal of driving licence, removal of passport or committal to prison. There is a good deal of overlap between the various checklists as the preliminary stages are the same for all of the applications.

1. Liability Order obtained. The checklist notes that it is a precondition for an application for disqualification (driving licence or passport) and committal.

2. Confirmation of enforcement attempt. The magistrates are asked to confirm, or have it demonstrated to them, that there has been an attempt by CMS/CSA to enforce the liability order either by a Warrant of Control (Bailiff action) or the use of the debt collection mechanisms in the County Court pursuant to section 36 of the Act. If some money has been recovered as a result of this process(es) then the outstanding balance should be noted. If the court is not satisfied that both of the above stages have been properly completed, then the checklist advises that the application should be dismissed.

3. Enquiry in the presence of the PP/NRP as to need for passport/driving licence, means and whether there has been wilful refusal or culpable neglect.

    a. The checklist notes that it is for CMS/CSA to adduce sufficient evidence to establish a case to answer that at some point since making the liability order the PP/NRP has had the means to make payments in respect of the liability order debt. It is suggested that this should not be a particularly elaborate task.

b. While noting that there is no requirement for evidence to be served in advance of the hearing a failure to do so may raise a question as to whether or not the PP/NRP is taken by surprise such as to undermine his Article 6 rights. Failing to do so risks an application for an adjournment which it would be very hard to resist. In practice CMS/CSA will have served a bundle of evidence including information in respect of the PP/NRP's finances (usually an analysis of his bank account over several months) demonstrating that there is "discretionary expenditure" some of which could be used to pay child support.

c. A note in the checklist correctly makes it clear that it is not for the PP/NRP to show cause why the sanction should not be imposed (forgive the double negatives). It is for CMS/CSA to demonstrate to criminal standard of proof that there has been a "wilful refusal" or a "culpable neglect" to pay.

d. "Wilful refusal" is the deliberate defiance of the court order and includes those situations where the defaulter refuses to pay on a point of principle.

e. "Culpable neglect" is a reckless disregard of a court order and include situations where the defaulter has chosen to use his income for non-essential items in preference to paying what is owed. Culpable neglect cannot be found when the defaulter has no income or capital with which to pay.

f. The checklist specifically notes that if there is a prima facie case that the PP/NRP has had means to pay then it is for him to rebut this. There is a shift in the evidential burden. It is noted, in paragraph 47 of *Karoonian* that this evidential shift is in no way objectionable and occurs every day in every court.

4. Further consideration of wilful refusal/culpable neglect. The checklists go on to note that in assessing whether there has been wilful refusal/culpable neglect the relevant time frame is the period after the making of the liability order. Conduct prior to the making of the liability order may be relevant insofar as it provides evidence of an attitude of mind from which inferences can be drawn as to the PP/NRP's attitude after the order was granted[30]. The advice specifically reiterates the position that, while it is an essential element of the application, providing the evidence to demonstrate wilful refusal/culpable neglect may not be particularly onerous given what has gone before. It also notes that there is absolutely no obligation upon the PP/NRP to give evidence.

5. Choice of sanction. On the assumption that the court has concluded that there has been wilful refusal or culpable neglect it then needs to consider what sanction to impose. The legislation specifically requires the court to enquire as to whether the PP/NRP needs their passport or driving licence for their work. In *Karoonian*[31] it is suggested that this means he should not be deprived of his passport/driving licence so that he can continue to earn (and pay). It is noted that CMS/CSA should make representations as to what sanction is preferable. The author would suggest that the essential decision before the court is which sanction is most likely to result in the payment of the outstanding maintenance. This will always depend on an assessment of the individual. In the author's personal experience some PPS/NRP's are terrified about going to prison while others are wholly nonplussed. Similarly in relation to loss of driving licence, some regard this with considerable trepidation while another merely

30 This is specifically envisaged in paragraph 24 of *Karoonian.*

31 At paragraph 28.

remarked that it would mean his chauffeur would have to work a little harder.

   a. The checklists make it clear that reasons should be given for the choice of one sanction as opposed to another. Identifying the reason or reasons should be relatively straightforward and may be quite brief.

6. Immediate or suspended/postponed. The legislation makes it clear that the court has the discretion to delay the implementation of the sanction on any terms it sees fit. The word "suspend" and its variants are used in the sections in relation to passport and driving licence, in relation to custody the word used is "postpone". The checklists in relation to passport and driving licence say that the penalty should only be suspended for a maximum of six months and that a specific date must be given for the imposition of the penalty. It suggests that these orders are not for long term instalment plans but for full payment. There is reference to the statutory forms for the orders, however this provision is out of date as the use of prescriptive forms has been repealed[32].

7. Amount/part payment. If a sanction is imposed details should be given of the amount outstanding. If payment is made in full then the PP/NRP is entitled to make an application to court for the immediate removal of the sanction. If a sanction has been postponed or suspended and part payment has been made, then the court should consider reducing the original penalty to take account of the partial payment.

[32] The explanatory forward to the repealing legislation makes it clear that in the digital age use of prescriptive paper forms is outdated and not cost-effective. It is suggested that if some form of record is required this should be derived from the court register – so potentially quite a lot depends on the accuracy of the record made by the legal adviser of the proceedings.

a. If prior to the implementation date of a suspended or postponed penalty the PP/NRP has discharged the debt in full then they, or any other interested party may make an application to the court for the discharge of the penalty. The discharge is not automatic.

8. The consequence of the need to give a specific date for the implementation of any penalty in relation to passport or driving licence and the six-month backstop suggested by the checklists means that the choice of sanction may default to committal as there is no requirement in the checklist, in relation to committal, to give a specific date. The checklists say that there is no specific upper limit to the length of the postponement of a committal order but notes that the *Karoonian* decision suggested that it should seldom exceed two years. The checklist suggests that if the debt cannot be discharged in two years that the court should seek some alternative means of enforcement. However, at the moment, there are no alternative means of enforcement in relation to sanctions so it would appear that, given the absence of alternatives, an extended period of postponed committal becomes the only option.

The requirement for a specific date in relation to the disqualification options is not set out in the statute or regulations. It would appear to be an operational construct by the authors of the checklist. While the setting of time limits may accord with other areas where a suspended / postponed or deferred penalty is put in place there must be a question as to on what statutory basis it is imposed in relation to unpaid child maintenance (particularly as the obligation to pay child maintenance is in a very limited class of debts which are not subject to insolvency proceedings and appear to remain payable to one's grave, and indeed beyond.)

The checklists have various breaks to allow the magistrates to make particular findings and to give particular reasons for the various decisions necessary to determine the application. It is to be hoped that these findings and reasons are fully recorded by the legal adviser in the court register. In that the court register is now the main record as to the proceedings advocates for both the applicant and the respondent should take care to ensure that the appropriate notes are made of the justices' decisions. All the more so as such hearings will usually be conducted in front of lay magistrates who are often inexact in the terminology that they use.

Both the provisions in relation to removal of driving licence and removal of passport provide that the court making an order "shall" require the person to whom it relates to produce their travel document / passport or driving licence to the court. There is no specific provision as to when exactly the documents should be produced. If the order is suspended the implication would be that the documents should be produced when the order is due to come into effect. Given that there is the use of the word "shall" this would indicate that the provision is mandatory and should be dealt with at the time the order is put into place even if it is on a suspended basis.

Failure to comply with terms of suspension or postponement

In general, even if findings of wilful refusal or culpable neglect have been made the imposition of any sanction will have been suspended or postponed on agreed terms. If the PP/NRP does not comply with the terms of the suspended arrangement what happens next? The legislation is perhaps not as explicit as it might be. Section 40.11.b provides that the Secretary of State shall have the power to make regulations allowing an application under section 40 "*to be renewed where no warrant is issued or term of imprisonment is fixed*". Section 40B.11 provides that the Secretary of State may make provisions in relation to disqualification orders corresponding to section 40.11. Section 39F contains a similar provision in relation to applications to remove passports. The relevant regulations are 33, 35 and 35A and provide that the application can be renewed on the ground that the circumstances of the liable person have changed. These provide a mechanism for the PP/NRP who is in default of the terms of the postponement/suspension of the sanction to be brought back before the court. It is an open question as to whether or not it would be necessary to repeat the findings and process in relation to the liability order, enforcement, means enquiry, need for passport and/or driving licence in order to earn one's living, and whether there has been wilful refusal or culpable neglect. In that the imposition of a sanction, even on a suspended or postponed basis requires that these steps have been taken it might be argued that the court should simply endorse the previous findings and impose whatever penalty it thinks just.

There is authority to suggest, in a case involving unpaid community charge (a forerunner of the council tax), that where there has already been a determination as to whether or not to issue a warrant of commitment, but it has been postponed on the basis of payments being made and those payments were not made that, provided the defaulter has had notice of a subsequent hearing to consider issuing the warrant of commitment, it is permissible to issue the warrant in his absence[33].

Fourth section in the checklists which deals with non-compliant orders

We are not quite done with the JCS checklist. After the sections dealing with loss of driving licence, passport or committal there is a further section dealing with "Non-compliant orders". As we have seen the usual outcome for a sanctions hearing is that there is a finding and the imposition of a penalty which is suspended or postponed. It is possible that cases will come before the court where the PP/NRP has failed to comply with the terms of the suspension/postponement and the court will be asked to consider whether or not to implement the sanction. It is conceivable, if with the passage of time increasingly unlikely, that the initial hearing imposing the suspended/postponed penalty was defective because of a failure to comply with the post *Karoonian* procedures.

The legal advisers are invited to check that the procedures and formalities in relation to the original hearing have been complied with properly and that all of the relevant statutory conditions and actions had taken place.

---

33 [1992] 7 WLUK 390 | (1993) 157 J.P. 869 | [1992] R.A. 283 | (1993) 157 J.P.N. 490 | (1993) 157 L.G. Rev. 801 | Times, September 18, 1992 | Independent, September 4, 1992

In the event that there is any defect then the order is a nullity and the application to enforce should be dismissed and CMS/CSA invited to submit a new, compliant, application.

The checklist envisages that if the process is defective but that the PP/NRP is in court it may be appropriate to conduct a replacement hearing at once. Obviously, there may be some evidential difficulties in presenting to the court evidence of the PP/NRP's finances and the relevant documentation to confirm the making of the liability order and the necessary attempts to enforce it. Moreover, it may be questionable as to whether the PP/NRP has had reasonable time to prepare and obtain legal advice if he wished.

This section of the checklist also references the cases referred to in the *Newham v Stratford Magistrates* decision referred to above in relation to the setting aside of civil orders in Magistrates' Courts.

<u>Other matters in relation to sanctions hearings</u>

Section 40B (Disqualification from driving: further provision) provides specifically that the court shall not take action in relation to it and section 40 (Commitment to prison) at the same time. There is a similar provision within the wording of section 39B (Disqualification for holding or obtaining UK passport) prohibiting action under this section and section 40. The court is not to apply two sanctions at the same hearing. However, by virtue of section 40B.7, it is made clear that the Secretary of State can make a further application under section 39A (Commitment to prison and disqualification from driving) if, when a period of disqualification which has been imposed, expires the monies identified as being outstanding when the order was imposed have not been paid in full. A follow-on application for potential for committal to prison and or removal of driving licence is perfectly permissible. If the removal of passport option has been used and the debt has not been paid in full when the sanction expires section 39C.5 provides that a further application to remove passport may be made. There is no follow-on provision within the wording of section 40. However, if there was further evidence of ability to pay and wilful refusal / culpable neglect there does not appear to be any statutory bar to making a further committal application even after a term of imprisonment has been served. Given the sensitivity about the use of committal to prison in respect of civil debt (notwithstanding it is in relation to the maintenance of the child) any follow-on application seeking a further period of committal to prison should be carefully scrutinised to ensure that the evidence relied upon postdates the original committal application / hearing.

We have seen above that the JCS checklists prescribed that specific dates and periods should be identified in relation to suspension of the imposition of penalties involving the removal of driving licence or travel document. That being said it could be argued that the appropriate "date" should be when the outstanding liability order debt is paid in full. It may well be that the issue as to whether a specific day or a specific eventuality is the appropriate "date" in relation to the discharge / implementation of any suspended or postponed penalty will be a matter considered by the appellate courts.

A final word

When appearing in a sanctions case and a suspended or postponed penalty has been imposed the author always says in court that the PP/NRP should be proactive in the event that they are unable to comply with the terms of the arrangement. It is the author's experience that CMS/CSA is generally very accommodating in the event that somebody's financial circumstances change (they lose their job or have an accident) and this means they are unable to comply with the arrangement. If, however, the PP/NRP makes an arrangement and then immediately breaks it CMS/CSA is likely to pursue the matter vigorously and the court is likely to have very little sympathy with the defaulter.

Top tips

1. If acting for CMS, try and make sure that there is a single paginated bundle available for the court and the respondent. It is not unusual for CMS/CSA to prepare a bundle but have it split into several files and referenced as exhibits, some of which will be a single page while others may have multiple pages.

2. Check the date of the liability order.

3. Check the date of the certificate of Nulla bona and ensure that it post-dates the liability order.

4. Ensure that there is evidence of enforcement action (by Bailiff / warrant of control, third-party debt order or charging order) for each liability order in respect of which a sanctions application is being made. It is by no means unusual for CMS/CSA to seek sanctions in respect of several liability orders at the same time.

5. Review the analysis of the PP/NRP's bank statements / financial records to ensure that they postdate the liability order and that there is evidence of discretionary spending which could have been used to pay child maintenance.

6. Look to see if there is any evidence of payments of child support within the analysis of the banking records.

7. If acting for a respondent consider whether it is worthwhile challenging the financial analysis. In some cases assumptions are made about income and expenditure asserting that they are for the benefit of the PP/NRP when in in fact the PP/NRP has no beneficial interest in the transaction and he is, say, receiving money for payment to subcontractors (or something similar).

8. See if the PP/NRP has been making any payments of child support (it may be a long way short of what he has been assessed to pay) as

this could be evidence that he is trying to make payments that simply lacks the resources to pay all he should. Such evidence might call into question whether he is either neglecting to pay or wilfully refusing to pay.

9. If you are acting for the PP/NRP and the cases in a bulk list on a non-CPS court or there is a real possibility there will be insufficient court time to deal with a contested hearing it may be that, provided the PP/NRP is prepared to start paying something that an adjournment can be negotiated on the basis that the PP/NRP commences regular payments. CMS/CSA is more likely to accept such an adjournment if there is a lump sum payment as well as a commitment to regular payments. If CMS/CSA are determined to seek a finding (of wilful refusal/culpable neglect) and the imposition of a sanction it might be that you ask the court for an adjournment on that basis suggesting that some sort of formal finding in respect of the PP/NRP might have an adverse impact on his livelihood or family circumstances.

10. Be aware that the PP/NRP needs to understand that if he enters into some form of arrangement and fails to comply without good reason this will be further evidence of wilful refusal or culpable neglect upon his part. If there is good reason then it should be brought to the attention of CMS/CSA as soon as possible and it may well be that they are sympathetic.

11. In that proceedings in the Magistrates' Court are not routinely recorded and the use of statutory forms has been repealed, the court record assumes greater importance and so in relation to any particular decision or reason or finding an advocate may wish to rely upon at a later date it would be prudent to slow the pace of one's delivery to ensure that accurate notes are made by the legal adviser. Indeed, confirming specific wording could eliminate confusion in the future.

12. Ensure that a reason is given for the choice of any sanction imposed.

13. If acting for a PP/NRP who is subject to a suspended/postponed passport/driving licence penalty it is important to remind them that the penalty will come into force on the date notified by the court and if they make payment in full that they need to make an application to the court to revoke the penalty. If this is not done the danger is that the PP/NRP may be driving without a licence or get stuck at passport control with an invalid travel document.

14. Given that lay magistrates are often quite imprecise in the language that they use advocates should be ready to assist them in tidying up their language and decision so that it mirrors the statutory wording and ensures that the appropriate preliminary findings are made and the reasons for any conclusion are recorded.

15. If one is instructed to deal with a case where the PP/NRP has failed to comply with the terms of suspension or postponement it would be prudent to be in a position to effectively argue the application from the beginning. If representing the PP/NRP and there is some good reason for the failure to comply with the terms of suspension/postponement then it would be wise to have the relevant evidence available for the court as it is unlikely to be patient or grant an adjournment without compelling reason.

CHAPTER TEN

COUNTY COURT HEARINGS

We have already seen how the making of a liability order against a PP/NRP and that an attempt has been made to enforce the debt either by a Warrant of Control (Bailiff action) or by use of the debt enforcement tools of the County Court is a precondition of an application for sanctions. There is also scope for the PP/NRP to challenge the enforcement actions in the County Court.

Once a liability order has been obtained CMS/CSA will register the Notice of Award with the County Court. This is an administrative process. CMS/CSA usually take the opportunity to write to the PP/NRP about the registration in the hope that it will trigger engagement from them and lead to the payment of maintenance. Sometimes PP/NRPs or what we might term pseudo lawyers advising them will seek to challenge this administrative process, but such submissions usually get short shrift from the Court.

The two main tools enforcement tools are a Third-Party Debt Order or a Charging Order. The procedures in relation to these orders have been streamlined in recent years in order to minimise the use of judicial time on what are effectively rubberstamped applications.

While CMS/CSA does occasionally use Third Party Debt Order in the author's experience these are relatively rare occurrences, and it is difficult to discern any generic advice in relation thereto as they will be very fact specific in relation to the debtor owing the PP/NRP the money potentially subject to the order.

The situation in relation to charging orders is rather different. Interim charging orders will be issued on a without notice basis, and it is only if the PP/NRP objects to the making of a final charging order that the matter will fall to be dealt with in the local county court.

If the PP/NRP appears as a legal owner of the property on the HM Land Registry search the presumption will be that they have a beneficial interest in the property and so this may be targeted by CMS/CSA in the event that there is a child maintenance debt outstanding.

It may well be the case that the PP/NRP is the joint owner of the family home with the RP/PwC. If the property has not yet been dealt with in ancillary relief proceedings (or otherwise) in the Family Court then notwithstanding that the PP/NRP is no longer resident at the property that he retains a legal and beneficial interest. It is by no means unusual for CMS/CSA to seek a charging order over such an interest whilst the RP/PwC continues to be in occupation of the property with the qualifying children.

The test for obtaining a charging order is very low. The court is not being asked to make a determination at the hearing as to whether or not the PP/NRP has a beneficial interest in the property. (Though this will become a material question if CMS/CSA seeks an order for sale having already obtained a charging order.) In general, it is very difficult to resist the making of a Final Charging Order unless there is clear documentary evidence establishing that the PP/NRP has no beneficial interest. This does sometimes happen. Some PP/NRP's enter into new relationships and because they are in occupation of the property which is actually purchased and owned by their new partner are expected to be named on the mortgage and on the title deeds by any lender. Because they are aware that they are potentially subject to enforcement action in respect of unpaid child maintenance debt they are astute enough to ensure that they enter into a deed of trust in relation to the ownership of the property making it clear that they have no beneficial interest. The author has seen cases where such deeds of trust have rolled on from one property to another as the PP/NRP and his new partner move to new houses.

If there is such a deed of trust, and there are no questions as to its authenticity, it is very difficult for CMS/CSA to challenge the validity of such a document. If this is an issue in respect of the case in which you are instructed then if you are acting for the PP/NRP it would be sensible to write to CMS/CSA providing them with a copy of the trust documentation and inviting them to dismiss the application. If no response is received then there should be at least one chaser letter, preferably more, both sent by the CMS portal and hardcopy. If multiple steps have been taken to bring the issue to the attention of CMS/CSA and yet the hearing has proceeded and the application for a final charging order has been lost then the scope for obtaining an order for costs is significantly enhanced.

If acting on behalf of CMS/CSA in such a case where this issue has been raised, it would be sensible to have urgent in conversation with the Court Presenting Officer / case manager to identify whether there was any reason to believe that the trust documentation was invalid. If there is no basis for challenging the documentation, then it would almost certainly be prudent to withdraw the application unless there is compelling evidence to undermine the PP/NRP's case (and it is quite hard to see what such evidence would be). It is sometimes the position that if the PP/NRP is one of those individuals determined to avoid paying any child maintenance and is prepared to arrange his affairs to try and limit the scope of CMS/CSA to mount a successful enforcement action against him, that case officers can be overzealous. In such a situation it is the advocate's duty to warn them of the difficulties in pursuing the case and to explain that evidentially unsupported assertions that the PP/NRP is simply trying to avoid his liabilities are unlikely to persuade a court to grant a final charging order.

Top tips

1. Obtain an up-to-date HM land registry search and ascertain whether there are any deeds of trust or notices of beneficial interest recorded in relation to the property.

CHAPTER ELEVEN

OTHER "DEFENCES" AND ISSUES ARISING IN CHILD MAINTENANCE CASES

Insolvency

Upon occasion a PP/NRP may seek to avoid their child maintenance liability by threatening to make themselves bankrupt or enter into some other insolvency procedure (usually an Individual Voluntary Arrangement ("IVA")).

If the PP/NRP is really having difficulties with their debts then it may be that insolvency is the only option. However, it will not assist in relation to the child support debt. Monies owed to for child support are not debts which are provable in bankruptcy. This means that even if one is made bankrupt the obligation to pay the child support debt remains. The relevant statutory provision in relation to bankruptcy is rule 14.2.2.c[34] which states:

> *"(2) [Claims not provable] the following are not provable –*
>
> ...
>
> *(c) in bankruptcy –*
>
> ...

[34] Insolvency (England and Wales) Rules 2016

(iii) an obligation arising under a maintenance assessment made under the Child Support Act 1991"

The authority for the proposition that child maintenance debts are not provable in relation to an IVA is the appeal court case of *Child Maintenance and Enforcement Commission v Beesley & Whyman [2010] EWCA Civ 1344*.

Freeman of the land

The Internet can be a wonderful source of information enriching people's lives and knowledge. It can also be the complete opposite. Regrettably there are cases where individuals who are being pursued for unpaid child maintenance appear to have trawled the Internet for potential defences and alighted upon the "Freeman of the land". Essentially this is pseudo-mediaeval concept asserting that the relevant individual is not subject to any authority and as such cannot be required to pay child maintenance or comply with court orders. Unsurprisingly this attitude rarely finds favour with the court and is usually a passport to orders being made against the individual concerned.

US commercial code

This is a similar pretext whereby individuals quote various sections of US commercial code in the hope that it will avoid them having to pay child maintenance. Sometimes they talk of bills of exchange or issuing their own cheques or money. The author remembers one occasion when a respondent attended court and presented a variation on this argument. Unfortunately, the legal adviser, who was extremely knowledgeable about various aspects of corporate law asked the individual if he was purporting to issue money. When he said yes, she explained that to do so without authorisation under the Banking Act was potentially an offence which could result in imprisonment and asked him to reconsider, he did. The order was granted.

Access to children

An argument which the author has slightly more sympathy with is the situation where the PP/NRP is not paying child maintenance because the RP/PwC is preventing or restricting his access to the children. Questions about access are of course primarily a matter for the Family Court and so have no impact on the obligation to pay child maintenance. If acting for or against an individual in these circumstances the author has found it helpful if a gentle conversation is had with the individual and it is emphasised that a failure to pay child support will usually be detrimental to their being able to obtain access to the children.

It is also sometimes said that the RP/PwC has required the PP/NRP to make payments to her in cash rather than through CMS/CSA and used access to the children as a means of compelling this course of action. It is almost impossible for the lawyers involved in such case to know definitively whether such pressure has been applied but again gently pointing out that if you have been directed to pay monies to a statutory body such as CMS/CSA choosing to ignore this instruction is unlikely to end well. Usually this brings home to them the need to engage with CMS/CSA.

When the author is acting in such cases he often finds it instructive to put it to the Court Presenting Officer that the PP/NRP may well be minded to raise this issue in the proceedings and to see if it is possible to canvass the attitude of the RP/PwC to giving evidence as to what has happened (i.e. denying the cash payments). Usually, but by no means always, the RP/PwC is eager to assist. In cases where the RP/PwC is equivocal it may well be that CMS/CSA can be persuaded to adjourn the hearing for the matter to be investigated. It is important to note that the reason for someone being reluctant to give evidence does not necessarily mean that the PP/NRP is telling the truth. Some of the PP/NRPs in this situation (though thankfully a very small number) are quite extreme individuals of whom the RP/PwC is rightfully concerned about antagonising.

CHAPTER TWELVE

COMPLAINTS AND APPEALS

Appeals

As the reader will be aware from the material above the structure of child support legislation appears to be aimed at minimising the cost and expense of recovering money from absent fathers and limiting the opportunity of such individuals to appeal or challenge decisions in the courts.

If a PP/NRP believes that they have been assessed incorrectly then they will have a right to ask for a mandatory reconsideration of their case. If this reconsideration process does not yield a satisfactory result then they have a right of appeal to the Independent Appeals Tribunal. Similar rights apply to the RP/PwC if they believe that the level of assessment is too low.

In such cases it is very important for the person seeking to make the appeal that they comply with the relevant time limits and provide evidence to support their claim. The First-Tier Tribunal have a relatively extensive discretion to review the decision and can ask for the provision of a wide range of documentation. However, in coming to their decision, they are limited to considering evidence which would have been available at the time the decision-maker made the assessment under challenge. It is also the case that their decision will usually be limited to the period identified in the assessment.

It often takes many months for appeals to work their way through the system. The author was recently involved in appeal hearing in mid-2023 which dated back to a decision taking place in 2019. Obviously matters were somewhat delayed by the pandemic and its aftermath but it is quite possible for a year to pass before the appeal is heard, meaning that there will likely have been a new annual review of the maintenance calculation which may in turn trigger new rights for mandatory reconsideration and further appeal rights. Indeed, it is quite possible for someone to have several appeals in respect of different assessment periods outstanding at the same time. If the lay client is in this position, then it is important that even though the first appeal has not been resolved that they ensure that they protect their position in respect of any follow-on periods by promptly exercising their rights to a mandatory reconsideration/appeal.

Complaint

The parties can also complain about the decisions taken by CMS/CSA. This process can run in parallel with the mandatory reconsideration and appeal to the First-Tier Tribunal. However, making a complaint and awaiting a response does not stop the clock running in relation to the time limits for making appeals.

If the initial response to the complaint is unsatisfactory then the aggrieved party can ask for the matter to be considered by the Independent Case Examiner. As the name suggests this is an independent official who should scrutinise the case to see if there has been any error or poor service. If there has been some error or fault this may result in the payment of compensation though the quantum of any payment is usually pretty trivial.

Complain to your MP

It is also open to PP/NRPs and RP/PwCs to complain to their MPs about how CMS/CSA has handled their case. CMS/CSA has a special unit which deals with Parliamentary correspondence. This can be a surprisingly effective tool in ensuring that a case is properly considered by someone with a degree of discretion and practicality. Civil servants, and CMS/CSA is part of the DWP, tend to be concerned about being subject to Parliamentary scrutiny and will treat an MP's representations with a good deal of care. Sadly, some MPs are much better than others at representing the interests of their constituents but if the lay client feels aggrieved it is certainly worth a letter to the MP asking them to raise the matter with the DWP/CMS/CSA.

Subject access request

If the PP/NRP or the RP/PwC is seeking evidence for their complaint or an appeal then they have a right under the Data Protection Act 2018 to request a copy of the documents held by CMS/CSA in respect of them. This can be a very useful tool in determining what information may have been utilised by CMS/CSA in making the maintenance calculation in respect of their case. Material relating to the other parent will be redacted but this disclosure could well provide useful evidence to establish that a mistake has been made in relation to the case. It can also show the extent to which historic records are available and may provide some illumination as to the decision-making process within CMS/CSA.

It appears that in responding to a Subject Access Request ("SAR") a search is conducted of CMS/CSA records and copies of the relevant material provided to the data subject. CMS/CSA does not keep a copy of the material that it supplies to the data subject, and each search for relevant documentation, if it is a case with a reasonably lengthy history, is a one-off exercise and can yield different results.

Getting a SAR answered can take months but does not stop the time running in respect of any deadlines. There is a reasonable chance that any complaint or appeal will take many weeks if not months to get going so there is likely to be a window for submitting additional information arising from the SAR before there is a substantive consideration of the complaint or appeal. Indeed, it can also be stated in the complaint or appeal that the party is awaiting a SAR and reserves the right to provide additional information once it is received.

CMS portal

In theory PP/NRPs and RP/PwCs should be able to access all the relevant documentation to their case via the CMS portal. It should also be possible to upload documents and correspondence and communications via this mechanism.

Readers will not be surprised to hear that quite a number of the PP/NRPs who come before the courts have not set up or fully utilised the portal in respect of their case. While large IT projects associated with government departments are frequently beset with difficulties, it would be prudent for parents involved with the CMS/CSA to try and use the portal to manage their case.

As in all things involving government and litigation keeping copies of documents and chasing up letters and other communication is important. If a letter or communication is not responded to then follow-ups and chasers need to be sent. If there is a persistent failure to respond, then complaints need to be made both to CMS/CSA but also to your MP or direct to the Secretary of State. It is important to be sensible and reasonable. While the initial audience for such communication is CMS/CSA the ultimate audience may be the court. The objective is to be able to produce a body of evidence of someone acting reasonably to raise a serious issue and being badly treated. The thing to avoid is being perceived as crossing the line from diligent and assiduous pursuit of a reasonable issue or complaint and becoming instead a harasser or stalker. The author is aware of some instances where CMS/CSA has used the provisions of the Harassment Act 1997 to curtail the activities of some PP/NRPs and RP/PwCs.

Top tips

1. Act promptly, the deadlines for requesting mandatory reconsideration and exercising appeal rights are very strict and in most cases are impossible to extend (even if the tribunal might wish to do so).

2. Keep copies, read receipts, delivery notifications and the like in respect of all communications with CMS/CSA. In respect of material sent to CMS/CSA prepare certificates of service or send it recorded delivery. This is simply a written notice that something has been sent by first-class post to the relevant party giving details of how it was sent.

MORE BOOKS BY LAW BRIEF PUBLISHING

A selection of our other titles available now:-

'A Practical Guide to Estate Administration and Crypto Assets' by Richard Marshall
'A Practical Guide to Managing GDPR Data Subject Access Requests – Second Edition' by Patrick O'Kane
'A Practical Guide to Parental Alienation in Private and Public Law Children Cases' by Sam King QC & Frankie Shama
'Contested Heritage – Removing Art from Land and Historic Buildings' by Richard Harwood QC, Catherine Dobson, David Sawtell
'The Limits of Separate Legal Personality: When Those Running a Company Can Be Held Personally Liable for Losses Caused to Third Parties Outside of the Company' by Dr Mike Wilkinson
'A Practical Guide to Transgender Law' by Robin Moira White & Nicola Newbegin
'A Practical Guide to 'Stranded Spouses' in Family Law' by Mani Singh Basi
'A Practical Guide to Residential Freehold Conveyancing' by Lorraine Richardson
'A Practical Guide to Pensions on Divorce for Lawyers' by Bryan Scant
'A Practical Guide to Challenging Sham Marriage Allegations in Immigration Law' by Priya Solanki
'A Practical Guide to Legal Rights in Scotland' by Sarah-Jane Macdonald
'A Practical Guide to New Build Conveyancing' by Paul Sams & Rebecca East
'A Practical Guide to Defending Barristers in Disciplinary Cases' by Marc Beaumont
'A Practical Guide to Inherited Wealth on Divorce' by Hayley Trim
'A Practical Guide to Practice Direction 12J and Domestic Abuse in Private Law Children Proceedings' by Rebecca Cross & Malvika Jaganmohan
'A Practical Guide to Confiscation and Restraint' by Narita Bahra QC, John Carl Townsend, David Winch
'A Practical Guide to the Law of Forests in Scotland' by Philip Buchan
'A Practical Guide to Health and Medical Cases in Immigration Law' by Rebecca Chapman & Miranda Butler

‘A Practical Guide to Bad Character Evidence for Criminal Practitioners by Aparna Rao

‘A Practical Guide to Extradition Law post-Brexit’ by Myles Grandison et al

‘A Practical Guide to Hoarding and Mental Health for Housing Lawyers’ by Rachel Coyle

‘A Practical Guide to Psychiatric Claims in Personal Injury – 2nd Edition’ by Liam Ryan

‘Stephens on Contractual Indemnities’ by Richard Stephens

‘A Practical Guide to the EU Succession Regulation’ by Richard Frimston

‘A Practical Guide to Solicitor and Client Costs – 2nd Edition’ by Robin Dunne

‘Constructive Dismissal – Practice Pointers and Principles’ by Benjimin Burgher

‘A Practical Guide to Religion and Belief Discrimination Claims in the Workplace’ by Kashif Ali

‘A Practical Guide to the Law of Medical Treatment Decisions’ by Ben Troke

‘Fundamental Dishonesty and QOCS in Personal Injury Proceedings: Law and Practice’ by Jake Rowley

‘A Practical Guide to the Law in Relation to School Exclusions’ by Charlotte Hadfield & Alice de Coverley

‘A Practical Guide to Divorce for the Silver Separators’ by Karin Walker

‘The Right to be Forgotten – The Law and Practical Issues’ by Melissa Stock

‘A Practical Guide to Planning Law and Rights of Way in National Parks, the Broads and AONBs’ by James Maurici QC, James Neill et al

‘A Practical Guide to Election Law’ by Tom Tabori

‘A Practical Guide to the Law in Relation to Surrogacy’ by Andrew Powell

‘A Practical Guide to Claims Arising from Fatal Accidents – 2nd Edition’ by James Patience

‘A Practical Guide to the Ownership of Employee Inventions – From Entitlement to Compensation’ by James Tumbridge & Ashley Roughton

‘A Practical Guide to Asbestos Claims’ by Jonathan Owen & Gareth McAloon

‘A Practical Guide to Stamp Duty Land Tax in England and Northern Ireland’ by Suzanne O’Hara

‘A Practical Guide to the Law of Farming Partnerships’ by Philip Whitcomb

‘Covid-19, Homeworking and the Law – The Essential Guide to Employment and GDPR Issues’ by Forbes Solicitors

‘Covid-19 and Criminal Law – The Essential Guide’ by Ramya Nagesh

'Covid-19 and Family Law in England and Wales – The Essential Guide' by Safda Mahmood
'A Practical Guide to the Law of Unlawful Eviction and Harassment – 2nd Edition' by Stephanie Lovegrove
'Covid-19, Brexit and the Law of Commercial Leases – The Essential Guide' by Mark Shelton
'A Practical Guide to Costs in Personal Injury Claims – 2nd Edition' by Matthew Hoe
'A Practical Guide to the General Data Protection Regulation (GDPR) – 2nd Edition' by Keith Markham
'Ellis on Credit Hire – Sixth Edition' by Aidan Ellis & Tim Kevan
'A Practical Guide to Working with Litigants in Person and McKenzie Friends in Family Cases' by Stuart Barlow
'Protecting Unregistered Brands: A Practical Guide to the Law of Passing Off' by Lorna Brazell
'A Practical Guide to Secondary Liability and Joint Enterprise Post-Jogee' by Joanne Cecil & James Mehigan
'A Practical Guide to the Pre-Action RTA Claims Protocol for Personal Injury Lawyers' by Antonia Ford
'A Practical Guide to Neighbour Disputes and the Law' by Alexander Walsh
'A Practical Guide to Forfeiture of Leases' by Mark Shelton
'A Practical Guide to Coercive Control for Legal Practitioners and Victims' by Rachel Horman
'A Practical Guide to Rights Over Airspace and Subsoil' by Daniel Gatty
'Tackling Disclosure in the Criminal Courts – A Practitioner's Guide' by Narita Bahra QC & Don Ramble
'A Practical Guide to the Law of Driverless Cars – Second Edition' by Alex Glassbrook, Emma Northey & Scarlett Milligan
'A Practical Guide to TOLATA Claims' by Greg Williams
'A Practical Guide to Elderly Law – 2nd Edition' by Justin Patten
'A Practical Guide to Responding to Housing Disrepair and Unfitness Claims' by Iain Wightwick
'A Practical Guide to the Construction and Rectification of Wills and Trust Instruments' by Edward Hewitt
'A Practical Guide to the Law of Bullying and Harassment in the Workplace' by Philip Hyland

'How to Be a Freelance Solicitor: A Practical Guide to the SRA-Regulated Freelance Solicitor Model' by Paul Bennett
'A Practical Guide to Prison Injury Claims' by Malcolm Johnson
'A Practical Guide to the Small Claims Track – 2nd Edition' by Dominic Bright
'A Practical Guide to Advising Clients at the Police Station' by Colin Stephen McKeown-Beaumont
'A Practical Guide to Antisocial Behaviour Injunctions' by Iain Wightwick
'Practical Mediation: A Guide for Mediators, Advocates, Advisers, Lawyers, and Students in Civil, Commercial, Business, Property, Workplace, and Employment Cases' by Jonathan Dingle with John Sephton
'The Mini-Pupillage Workbook' by David Boyle
'A Practical Guide to Crofting Law' by Brian Inkster
'A Practical Guide to the Law of Domain Names and Cybersquatting' by Andrew Clemson
'A Practical Guide to the Law of Gender Pay Gap Reporting' by Harini Iyengar
'NHS Whistleblowing and the Law' by Joseph England
'Employment Law and the Gig Economy' by Nigel Mackay & Annie Powell
'A Practical Guide to Noise Induced Hearing Loss (NIHL) Claims' by Andrew Mckie, Ian Skeate, Gareth McAloon
'An Introduction to Beauty Negligence Claims – A Practical Guide for the Personal Injury Practitioner' by Greg Almond
'Intercompany Agreements for Transfer Pricing Compliance' by Paul Sutton
'Zen and the Art of Mediation' by Martin Plowman
'A Practical Guide to the SRA Principles, Individual and Law Firm Codes of Conduct 2019 – What Every Law Firm Needs to Know' by Paul Bennett
'A Practical Guide to Adoption for Family Lawyers' by Graham Pegg
'A Practical Guide to Industrial Disease Claims' by Andrew Mckie & Ian Skeate
'A Practical Guide to Redundancy' by Philip Hyland
'A Practical Guide to Vicarious Liability' by Mariel Irvine
'A Practical Guide to Applications for Landlord's Consent and Variation of Leases' by Mark Shelton
'A Practical Guide to Relief from Sanctions Post-Mitchell and Denton' by Peter Causton
'A Practical Guide to Equity Release for Advisors' by Paul Sams

'A Practical Guide to Financial Services Claims' by Chris Hegarty
'The Law of Houses in Multiple Occupation: A Practical Guide to HMO Proceedings' by Julian Hunt
'Occupiers, Highways and Defective Premises Claims: A Practical Guide Post-Jackson – 2nd Edition' by Andrew Mckie
'A Practical Guide to Financial Ombudsman Service Claims' by Adam Temple & Robert Scrivenor
'A Practical Guide to Running Housing Disrepair and Cavity Wall Claims: 2nd Edition' by Andrew Mckie & Ian Skeate
'A Practical Guide to Holiday Sickness Claims – 2nd Edition' by Andrew Mckie & Ian Skeate
'Arguments and Tactics for Personal Injury and Clinical Negligence Claims' by Dorian Williams
'A Practical Guide to Drone Law' by Rufus Ballaster, Andrew Firman, Eleanor Clot
'A Practical Guide to Compliance for Personal Injury Firms Working With Claims Management Companies' by Paul Bennett
'RTA Allegations of Fraud in a Post-Jackson Era: The Handbook – 2nd Edition' by Andrew Mckie
'RTA Personal Injury Claims: A Practical Guide Post-Jackson' by Andrew Mckie
'On Experts: CPR35 for Lawyers and Experts' by David Boyle
'An Introduction to Personal Injury Law' by David Boyle

www.ingramcontent.com/pod-product-compliance
Lightning Source LLC
LaVergne TN
LVHW022048200926
848481LV00003B/826
* 9 7 8 1 9 1 4 6 0 8 2 9 2 *